garden &
patio
living spaces

Consulting Editor: Don Vandervort

Staff for this Book:

Editor: Rob Lutes

Art Director: Odette Sévigny

Assistant Editor: Ned Meredith

Writer: Angelika Gollnow

Researcher: Adam van Sertima

Designer: Hélène Dion

Picture Editor: Linda Castle

Production Editor: Brian Parsons

Production Coordinator: Dominique Gagné

Systems Director: Edward Renaud

Scanner Operators: Martin Francoeur, Sara Grynspan

Technical Support: Jean Sirois

Indexer: Linda Cardella Cournoyer

Book Consultants:

Richard Ludwig

Timothy N. Thoelecke Jr.

Mary Woolley

Garden & Patio Living Spaces was produced in conjunction with
ST. REMY MULTIMEDIA

Cover:

Photographer: Phil Harvey

Photo Director: JoAnn Masaoka Van Atta

Landscape Architect: Ransohoff, Blanchfield, Jones, Inc.

Cover Designer: Vasken Guiragossian

VP, Editorial Director, Sunset Books:
Bob Doyle

4 5 6 7 8 9 0 QPD/QPD 9 8 7 6 5 4 3 2 1 0

ISBN 0-376-01597-7
Library of Congress Catalog Card Number: 98-86305
Printed in the United States

For additional copies of *Garden & Patio Living Spaces*, or any
other Sunset book, call 1-800-526-5111, or visit our
website at: www.sunsetbooks.com.

garden & patio living spaces

Sunset

Table of Contents

A Gallery of
OUTDOOR
LIVING SPACES

Today outdoor living means more than tending the garden and mowing the lawn. With a little creativity and planning, your yard can become a living space where you spend a great deal of your time. Whether this means bug-proofing a patio with screens or setting up an outdoor kitchen and dining area with all the amenities for entertaining will depend on the specific needs of your family. Whatever your intentions, this chapter contains a selection of successful garden and patio living spaces to excite your imagination and provide inspiration.

Rustic stone majestically defines the back of this sloping property. Candles on stands, strategically placed along the wall, lend a classical feel to the space.

On a small, tree-shaded deck just outside the back door, a built-in bench and a sea of colorful throw pillows create an inviting spot for lounging.

An updated version of the old-fashioned glider swing turns a once unused shady corner into the perfect place to chat with friends or relax with a good book.

For those who love to be surrounded by blooms and greenery year-round, an attached greenhouse in a sunny southern spot functions as outdoor space. Most attached greenhouses have foundations, sturdy framing, electricity, water, insulation, and double or triple thermal windows.

A sun-bleached arbor, teeming with climbing roses, provides a sense of enclosure while framing an inviting view of the patio and garden beyond.

High lattice screens give walls to this outdoor room while still allowing ample entry for breezes and sunlight.

A stately brick fireplace provides a dramatic backdrop for an evening under the stars. With fixtures in place for a grill, the fireplace doubles as a barbecue.

This outdoor room can be used in virtually any weather. Sliding glass doors and windows with screens keep it bug-free and—with the help of fans—promote cross breezes to keep the room cool in summer. A glass roof allows sun to heat the interior when it's chilly outside.

Even a simple bench can create a sense of place in your yard. Here, a large, flat rock caps a rustic retaining wall, creating a look with timeless appeal.

An outdoor room with elegant arched screens provides a perfect spot for formal dining: close enough to the outdoors to enjoy the evening air, but out of the wind and rain, and safe from bugs.

Ivy-covered lattice screens shield the view from a neighboring yard, and bring greenery and privacy to a small urban space.

With its solid roof, intricate, airy lattice panels, and views of the property's lush greenery, this charming space serves as an ideal outdoor living room.

Tucked behind a tall fence, this well-organized space offers homeowners an attractive place to carry on a favorite hobby—gardening.

Outdoor play areas can be places for family members of all ages. This children's space is well protected with a fence, trees, and an umbrella for extra shade. The integrated sandbox, level with the patio, is near enough to the house for easy supervision. When the youngsters are grown, the sand can be removed and the structure can serve as a planter.

Given dappled shading by surrounding trees and decorated distinctively with plants, sculptures, and rustic furniture, this enclosed space hints at the wide range of design options for outdoor rooms.

Surrounded by breathtaking views, this gazebo provides a stunning getaway that is set away from the home's main outdoor living space.

Varying patio levels, lattice screens, and overheads make this single space seem like many. The arched lattice overhead serves as an intimate dining space.

Containers are an attractive and
convenient way of introducing plants
and flowers to a patio environment.
Here, flowering vines are trained on
a wire trellis to make the most of
the limited space available.

Planning
YOUR OUTDOOR
LIVING SPACE

When designing your living space, careful planning is crucial to arriving at a result that both meets your needs and looks attractive. This chapter gives you the planning savvy to bring to life the dozens of ideas for outdoor spaces offered in the other chapters of this book. Before making any changes, you'll need to look realistically at the plants and structures in your yard right now and chart a general course of action to bring about changes that will benefit both you and your family. Also take into account climate conditions such as wind and sun, as well as the issues of grading and drainage that are crucial in dealing with wet weather. You'll also need to draw up a plan. A simple, effective method is explained starting on page 25. You may want the help of a professional for this or another task. Go to page 28 for information on how to retain the right pro for the services you need. Finally, a section of sample designs by a professional landscape designer will provide the most vital ingredient of all: inspiration.

Evaluating Your Needs

Many homeowners rush to make changes to their outdoor living spaces without thinking the changes through thoroughly. In colder climates, this tends to occur at the first sign of spring, when the prospect of outdoor living is a particularly exciting one. To avoid this mistake, as you begin planning your outdoor living space, answer two basic questions: 1. What are my personal needs? 2. How are the existing structures and layout of the space failing to meet them?

PERSONAL NEEDS

The most important aspect of any living space is how it meets the needs of the people who use it. Your outdoor environment will be most successful if it can accommodate the full range of activities enjoyed by your family. Talk with everyone who will spend time in the space, including friends, neighbors, and relatives. While your goal is not to design by committee, the people who know you and the space can be valuable sources of ideas and insightful critics of designs that seem solid but may not work. When planned well, one area should be able to serve many purposes. On the other hand, do not overlook aesthetic concerns. Your space should be pleasant to be in, and this will hinge largely on how it looks.

Some important planning concerns are discussed below. These will help you get a general idea of your needs and the type of living space that could best meet them. Most of these elements are addressed in greater detail later in this book.

Privacy: To what degree and in which areas do you want privacy? Whether it's an area for solitary leisure time or an intimate space for hosting dinner parties, you may want to screen this area from the view of others. Choosing an area that is naturally enclosed can save you the trouble of erecting structures like walls and fences. Since in colder climates outdoor entertaining is usually done during the growing season, privacy can also be furnished effectively with plants of all types, ranging from vines to evergreens. In warmer climates where outdoor entertaining is done year-round, you have even more planting options at your disposal.

Entertaining: What kind of entertaining do you generally do and how often? Is it casual or formal? As a rule, dining spaces should be located close to the house to reduce the distances you have to carry dishes and food. Also keep in mind the number of people who will usually be dining in the space and allow enough room for all of them to be seated comfortably. To steer clear of foul odors, be aware of where your neighbors store their garbage and locate eating spaces away from this area.

Views: Are there particular views around your yard you enjoy? Plan your living space to take best advantage of these views. You can strategically place plantings to frame a chosen view. Likewise, there may be a view that you want to screen out. This can be accomplished using evergreen trees or shrubs and other plantings or with a fence, a wall, or a screen. If a view cannot be blocked, you can place something in the landscape that directs your attention away from that point. And don't forget the view of the space from inside the house—you'll frequently be seeing it from there.

Noise: Undesirable noises from the street, neighbors, and playgrounds or even air conditioners or pool equipment can be controlled in several ways. Masonry walls, fences, and screens all do a good job at reducing neighborhood sounds. In larger spaces, masses of evergreens can be a great help. A moving water feature such as a fountain is also effective at diverting attention from unwanted sounds. As well, you can use layout to your advantage, targeting seldom-used areas as buffers between the main living space and the sources of undesired noise.

Other considerations: There are many other personal issues that may determine the type of space that will best serve your needs. If you have children, consider what sort of space will accommodate them today and whether that design can be modified to meet their future needs. If you have pets, you may want to avoid planting certain fragile plants. Also think about whether you will be adding on to your home in the near future and how that addition might affect your yard. In general, just think very carefully before putting shovel to earth, and make notes you can use when it comes time to make a final plan.

EXISTING STRUCTURES

A second important step in planning your outdoor space is to evaluate carefully the structures that already exist in your yard. The basic building block of most outdoor living spaces is a flat, solid patio or deck. The success of your project will hinge to a large extent on the quality and attractiveness of this surface. A patio or deck that is badly falling apart or long out of style may need replacing. If the patio is in reasonable condition or if it can be repaired at relatively little cost, it's certainly more cost-effective to stick with what's there. Another important factor is how long you plan to stay in your current home. If you know you're going to be there for the foreseeable future, installing a new patio or deck might not seem like an overly costly option. If, however, you plan to move within the next few years, repairing what's there is an economical alternative to starting over from scratch. The same goes for many of the other structures in the space. For more information on installing and repairing patios, consult Sunset's *Complete Patio Book*. For decks, see Sunset's *Complete Deck Book*.

Should you choose to rebuild your patio or deck and redesign your living space entirely, be sure to take into account the feel and character of your neighborhood and of the house itself. Talk with neighbors before carrying out any major changes.

If you've just moved into a new home and are considering remodeling the landscape, it is advisable to wait at least a year before doing so. This will allow you to see all the seasonal changes in the garden, get a feel for the space's microclimates, and give you time to see exactly how you will use the space outside.

Finally, let simplicity be your guiding principle. Complicated changes can become costly. If you want to make difficult renovations, it is usually well worth it to contact a design professional during the planning stages.

For a peaceful mid-morning break, nothing beats the tranquility of an outdoor room such as the one shown here. Hanging flower baskets add both a touch of color and fragrance.

Understanding Your Property's Climate

A good understanding of local climate conditions will help you select the right site and allow you to design an outdoor living space that can be enjoyed over the longest season possible.

For example, the wind patterns on your property may dictate the need for a barrier or fence for protection, while a high average rainfall might make a solid-patio roof a good addition to your design.

Your relation to the sun: Exposure to the sun is one of the most impor-tant factors in your enjoyment of a potential site. A site that faces north is cool because it rarely receives sun. An exposed south-facing location is warmer because, from sunrise to sunset, the sun never leaves it. The east side of a property is cooler, as it receives only morning sun. A space that faces west is often extremely hot because it receives the full force of the sun's afternoon rays, as well as harsh glare.

Another factor to consider is the sun's path during the year. As the sun passes over your house, it makes an arc that changes slightly every day (as shown in the illustration at the bottom of the page). Changes in the sun's path give longer days in the summer and shorter days in the winter, and they also alter the sun and shade patterns on your property.

Microclimates: It is very rare that you experience the same temperature as at the weather bureau. A reported temperature reading of 68°F means that a thermometer in

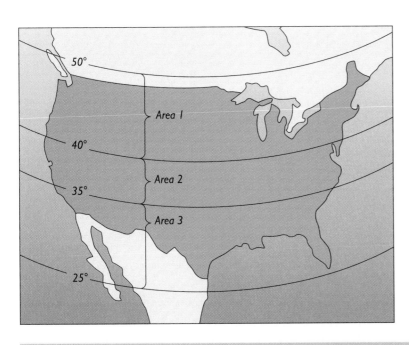

SUN AND SHADE

Sun and shade are cast at various angles, depending on the time of year and where you live. Find your location on the map at left, then refer to the chart below for the sun's angles and hours of daylight on your property.

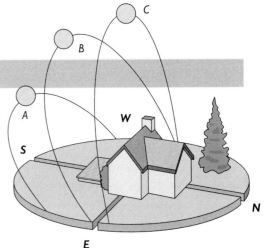

SUN IN YOUR YARD

SEASONAL SUN ANGLES

Time, Month/Day	Sun Angle/Hours of Daylight		
	Area 1	Area 2	Area 3
A Noon, 12/21	21°/8 hrs.	29°/9 hrs.	37°/10 hrs.
B Noon, 3/21 & 9/21	45°/12 hrs.	53°/12 hrs.	60°/12 hrs.
C Noon, 6/21	69°/16 hrs.	76°/15 hrs.	83°/14 hrs.

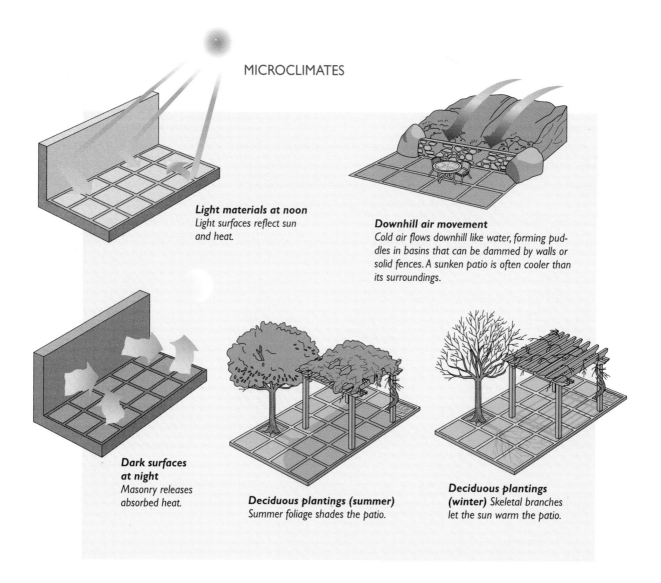

MICROCLIMATES

Light materials at noon
*Light surfaces reflect sun
and heat.*

Downhill air movement
*Cold air flows downhill like water, forming pud-
dles in basins that can be dammed by walls or
solid fences. A sunken patio is often cooler than
its surroundings.*

**Dark surfaces
at night**
*Masonry releases
absorbed heat.*

Deciduous plantings (summer)
Summer foliage shades the patio.

**Deciduous plantings
(winter)** *Skeletal branches
let the sun warm the patio.*

the shade protected from the wind reads 68°F. With a breeze of 10 to 15 miles per hour, a person in the shade will feel a temperature of about 62°F. Someone on a sunny, wind-sheltered patio, though, will experience a temperature that is a comfortable 75°F to 78°F.

The illustrations above show how design features and plantings can also create these localized pockets, or "microclimates."

Cold air flows downhill like water. It also "puddles" in basins and can be dammed by walls or solid fences. By building a sunken patio, you will create a space that may be pleasantly cool in a region where nights remain hot. However, in a climate where nights are cooler, you may find yourself shivering at sunset while higher surroundings remain quite balmy.

Certain materials reflect sun and heat better than others. For example, light colored masonry paving and walls are great at reflecting sun and heat, but they can be uncom-

fortably bright. Wood surfaces are usually cool. On the other hand, dark masonry materials retain heat longer, making your patio warmer in the evening (but possibly too hot during the day).

Plants help block the wind while letting breezes through. Deciduous trees (which lose their leaves in winter) that provide shade to a space during the hottest days of the summer will allow welcome rays of light to penetrate on crisp winter days.

Grading Land

Integral to designing your outdoor living space is observing the natural "lay of the land," specifically grading. Together with drainage considerations *(page 24)*, this will dictate to a large extent what you can construct and where. One significant advantage of decks over patios is that a deck allows you to have a flat outdoor space without changing the grading of your property.

A flat, level property lends itself to many more activities and construction possibilities than a sloped one, but on many sites changing the grade of land is necessary.

If your property lies on a slope so steep that without skillful grading and terracing it would remain unstable and virtually useless, consider constructing one or a series of retaining walls. The illustration below shows some examples of these techniques. The safest way to build the wall is to place it at the bottom of a gentle slope, if space permits, and fill in behind it with soil (option 1). Otherwise, the hill can be held either with a single high wall (option 2) or with a series of low retaining walls that form terraces (option 3).

If the grading is simple and you have the time and inclination to do the work, you can save money and have the satisfaction of literally shaping the land you'll live with for years to come. In tougher situations, such as lots requiring terracing or those that need a high retaining wall, it is recommended that you obtain professional help in the person of a contractor, landscape architect, or soil engineer. In these situations, a professional will be able to foresee potential problems and will be familiar with local legal requirements. In short, you should rely on the expertise of professionals for major grading, including the grading of any unstable areas.

Be aware that the cost of importing material for the fill is about four times the cost of having to take it away. Since soil compacts as it settles you will need to have approximately 20 percent more material than you think.

GRADING OPTIONS

Grading for steps and retaining walls requires cutting and filling. Several solutions are shown here. Retaining walls often require special drainage considerations. See page 24 for more information.

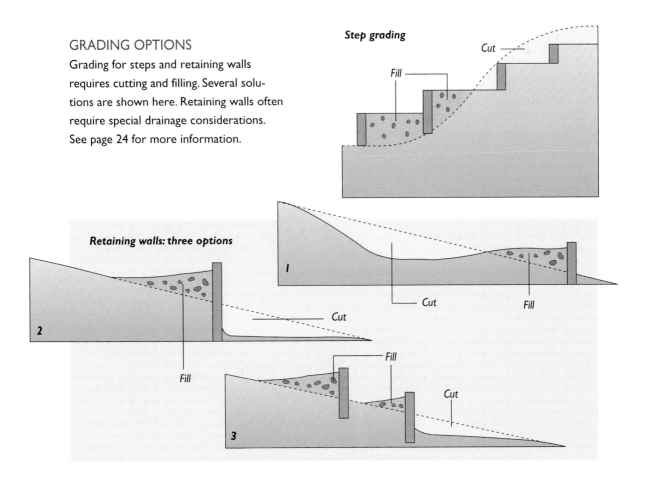

Step grading — Cut — Fill

Retaining walls: three options

1 — Cut — Fill

2 — Cut — Fill

3 — Fill — Cut

Drainage

Where you live will play a large role in how you need to approach the problem of drainage. If your climate is hot and dry, your property will need as much moisture as it can get. If your property is bombarded with heavy rainfall in the spring and summer months, however, you will most likely need to install drains. For efficiency, you should examine the possibility of providing for drainage at the same time as you assess your property for grading *(page 23)*. Drainage is especially important if you have decided to erect retaining walls. Excess water will buckle and damage retaining walls as well as any other structures you erect. Timber retaining walls allow water to pass through them naturally. Concrete walls, on the other hand, require "weep holes" in them or perforated drainpipe behind them.

If your landscape is nearly flat, it must have adequate surface drainage: a minimum slope of 1 inch per 8 feet of paved surface or about 3 inches per 10 feet of unpaved ground. Steeper gradients are better for slow-draining, heavy soils.

Always route water away from your house. A few ways of achieving this are shown below. Where the property slopes toward the house or any other fixed structure such as a gazebo or greenhouse, you'll probably have to shore up ground with a retaining wall, slope the surfaces inward, and direct runoff to a central drain. Another option is to build a swale, or low-lying area, to collect water and use a trench and drainpipe to route it away from the house. Rapid runoff from roofs and paved surfaces sometimes requires a special solution, such as drain tiles or a catch basin.

Steep slopes may drain fast enough to cause erosion. To retard erosion, such slopes need terracing and, sometimes, special structures. Ground covers and other plantings can also be used to slow runoff. A good horticultural mulch with particles of varying size will virtually eliminate the problem.

Percolation is the downward penetration of water into soil; it's extremely slow in clay soils, compacted surface soils, soils with mixed layers, and soils overlying hardpan. This is also a problem where the water table is close to the surface. Drainpipes or dry wells can often offer solutions; a major problem calls for a sump pump.

On steep clay slopes most water runs off, but retained water can cause mud slides. Get professional help to plan and install a drainage system for such steep hillsides.

DRAINING FOR SLOPES

A uniform slope *(right, top)* directs water away from the house; hilly yards and retaining walls may call for a central catch basin *(right, bottom)*; a swale directs water away from the house and into a trench where drainpipe carries it away from the property *(below)*.

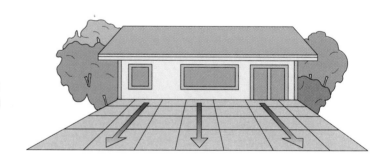

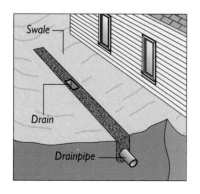

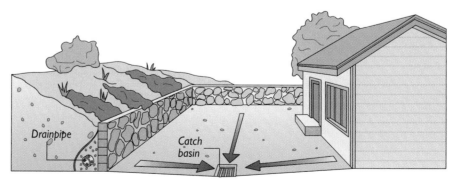

Planning Your Site

Reading through this book will give you dozens of ideas for creating garden and patio living spaces. The following information shows you how to put those ideas into a simple plot plan that will serve as your guide as you bring these ideas to life. Two rules of thumb will help you as you draw up your plan: 1. Be as precise as you possibly can; "guesstimates" or outright errors at this stage can result in disappointment later, when you find out, for example, that your greenhouse gets virtually no sun. 2. Exploring ideas by putting them down on paper is exciting and imaginative work. Enjoy it! You are not committing to anything at this stage and are free to explore any possibility you like. Let your imagination go and see what you come up with. You might surprise yourself.

DRAWING YOUR BASE MAP

The first step in making a plan for your living space is to draw a base map of your property. Use a large piece of graph paper (an 11- by 17-inch sheet with ¼-inch squares will be most convenient; very large lots may require a 24- by 36-inch sheet). You'll need a pencil, an eraser, a ruler, and tracing paper. Optional tools are a triangle, a compass, and a circle template. For measuring the landscape itself, use a 30- or 50-foot tape measure.

To draw your base map, assume each square on the graph paper represents one square foot on your living space (1 inch will equal 4 feet if you've used a ¼-inch grid graph paper). Starting with the dimensions of your property and proceeding through all the information listed here, you'll gradually be covering a good deal of your paper with written and sketched details, so make each entry neatly.

It is helpful, though by no means necessary, to have your deed map, house plans, or a contour map of your lot. If you don't have these at hand, see if they're available at your city hall, county office, title company, bank, or mortgage company.

The information listed below should appear in one form or another on your base map. Read through the list of measurements you'll need, then go outside and take them all in one trip.

Boundary lines and dimensions: Begin by outlining your property to scale and marking the relevant dimensions on the base map. It will be much easier to draw your plan if you position your property boundaries so the house is located along a line on the graph paper rather than at an angle to a line.

The house: Show your house to scale within the property. Note all doors to the outside and the direction that each opens, as well as the width of all lower windows and their height above ground. Note also the height of all overhangs.

Exposure: Draw an arrow pointing north with the help of a compass, then note on your base map any shaded and sunlit areas in the yard. Also note the microclimates—hot and cold spots and windy areas—that exist on the property. Indicate the direction of the prevailing wind and any spots that are especially windy and may require protection of some sort.

Utilities and easements: Show the locations of faucets and the depths and locations of all underground lines, including the sewage line or septic system, and all irrigation lines and heads. If you're contemplating installing a fence, planting a tree, or constructing a greenhouse, show the locations and heights of all overhead lines. If your deed map shows any easements, note them accurately on your base map and check restrictions limiting their development. If you aren't sure about the locations of any utilities and easements, call your local utility companies. They will often come to your property and indicate the locations of their lines.

Gradient: Note high and low points on the property. If drainage crosses boundaries, you may need to indicate the slope of adjacent properties as well to ensure that you're not channeling runoff onto your neighbor's property.

Drainage: Surface drainage corresponds to the slope of the land. Where does the water from paved surfaces drain? Note where drainage is impeded, leaving soil soggy, and whether runoff from steep hillsides is rapid enough to cause erosion.

Existing plantings and structures: If you plan to remodel an existing landscape, note the location of trees, plants, and all structural items you want to retain or that would require a major effort to remove.

Views: Note all views, attractive and unattractive, from every side of your property. Focus particularly on views from areas that will potentially be most used.

EXPERIMENTING WITH YOUR IDEAS

With your base map completed, you can now try out your ideas. There are a few fun and easy ways to do this. One technique is experimenting with "balloon sketches" *(page opposite)*. For each design attempt, use a separate sheet of tracing paper placed over your base map, sketching "balloons"— rough circles or ovals—to represent the location and approximate size of each use area. In lieu of using tracing paper, you can make copies of your base map and draw directly on them.

Another useful technique is using "to-scale" shapes. This involves cutting out a series of shapes to represent the different design elements you want to include in your living space. Place them in various locations on the plan, experimenting until you find the best locations for the elements you want to include.

Yet another planning method is to simply go into the space and take photos from various perspectives. Enlarge the photos using a photocopier, then draw in the various elements you're considering putting in the space.

Before you begin experimenting, however, it's important to go and spend time in the space and visualize different possible layouts. You can even cordon off areas or

A SAMPLE BASE MAP

A preliminary step in any landscaping project is to draw a base map—a scale drawing showing the important features and characteristics of the property.

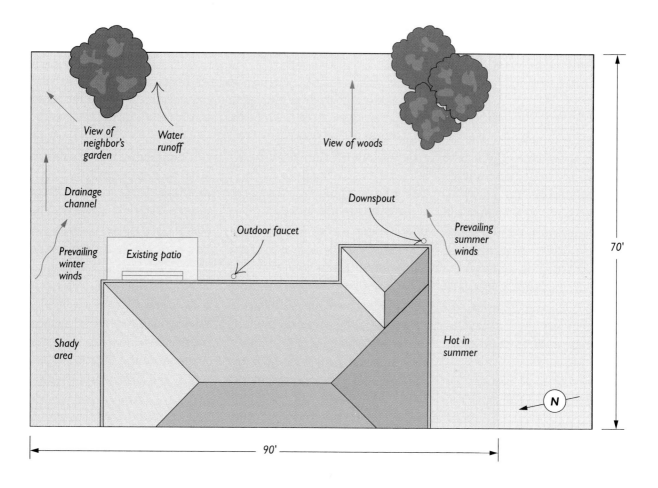

View of neighbor's garden

Water runoff

View of woods

Drainage channel

Downspout

Prevailing summer winds

Outdoor faucet

Prevailing winter winds

Existing patio

Shady area

Hot in summer

N

70'

90'

CREATING A BALLOON SKETCH

Place tracing paper over your base map, then draw circles for use areas and other features.

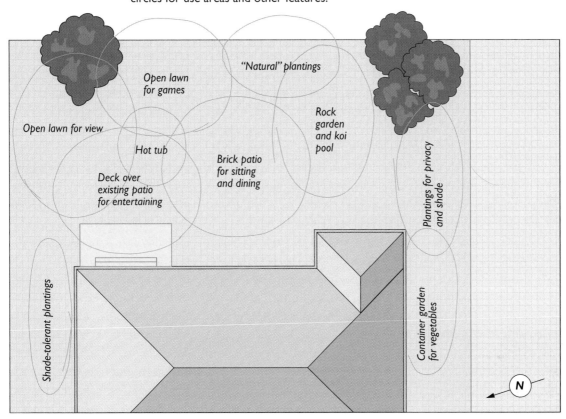

"Natural" plantings

Open lawn for games

Open lawn for view

Rock garden and koi pool

Hot tub

Brick patio for sitting and dining

Deck over existing patio for entertaining

Plantings for privacy and shade

Shade-tolerant plantings

Container garden for vegetables

N

use chairs or stakes to get a clearer idea of spaces and distances. Stand in proposed use areas and note all the views around you. Also walk through planned traffic paths.

Always try to see your design as a whole and as integrally connected to the inside of your home. For instance, if you plan to have an eating area shaded by an attached roof outside of your living room, will the roof make the living room dark?

Once you begin to put your ideas on paper, use familiar shapes as much as possible. Designs based on squares, rectangles, cir-

cles, and hexagons almost always generate results that are pleasing to the eye. Try to avoid arbitrarily curved patterns.

Make a list of planned use areas and keep it in front of you as you draw. Visualize foot-traffic connections between the various use areas as well as to and from the house. Will too much traffic be channeled through areas meant for relaxation? Can guests move easily from the entertaining area to the games area? Consider whether food can be easily transported from the kitchen to the barbecue and dining area.

DRAWING UP A FINAL PLAN

Once you've arrived at a design you are satisfied with, you're ready to draw up a final plan. This will be your visual guide as you go about making changes to your living space. Place a clean sheet of tracing paper directly over your base map (or use a fresh photocopy of your base map). Label all of the features, trying to keep in mind what your plan will look like in three dimensions and in color. Make the plan as neat and concise as possible. It not only is your map, but will serve as a guide for any contractors you hire.

Hiring a Professional

A number of professionals can help with the design and construction of your outdoor projects.

LANDSCAPE PROFESSIONALS

Landscape architects: With one or more degrees in their field, landscape architects are trained (and in many states licensed) to design both commercial and residential landscapes. They can help set objectives, analyze the site, produce detailed plans, and recommend contractors. Many are willing to give a simple consultation, either in their office or at your home, for a modest fee.

Landscape designers: Many landscape designers have a landscape architect's education and training. Though they are not licensed, they are often more experienced in residential projects and may have an art or horticulture background.

Professional engineers: Engineers can help with complicated grading and drainage considerations, and other site problems (unstable ground, steep lots, high winds).

Consulting engineers evaluate soil conditions and establish the design specifications for foundations, piers, and footings.

Landscape contractors: Landscape contractors are trained to install landscapes: plantings, pavings, structures, and irrigation systems. Some also offer design services.

Subcontractors: If you prefer to act as your own general contractor, you can hire and supervise skilled subcontractors. Subcontractors can usually supply you with current product information, sell fixtures and supplies, and do work according to technical specifications and local codes.

CHOOSING A PROFESSIONAL

The best way to choose a professional is through recommendations of friends and neighbors who have had work done that you can inspect for yourself. Collect the names of several contractors or subcontractors, and ask these companies for the names and phone numbers of a few of their clients. Call to find out if the jobs were done well.

Keep in mind that some excellent professionals have no professional affiliation, while many belong to the American Association of Landscape Architects (AALA), the American Institute of Architects (AIA), or the Association of Professional Landscape Designers (APLD).

If your project will cost over $5000, select three or four companies whose work you like and ask them to submit bids on a package you and your consultants have prepared (some contractors may decline to bid or will charge a fee, particularly on smaller projects). As the industry has few set regulations and standards, be sure you know exactly what you're getting if you accept the lowest bid. It's very easy for four companies to come up with four dramatically different bids, based on the scope of the project and the quality of materials used.

CONTRACT CONSIDERATIONS

Without a signed contract, you may have nothing but trouble. A contract is an agreement between two parties covering the performance of specified work for a certain amount of money.

A good contract protects both your interests and the builder's. It must describe everything to be done and by whom. Don't sign it until you understand all of it.

The contract should be on the contractor's professional letterhead, with the address of both the contractor and homeowner listed. It must be signed by both parties and should contain the following:

Plans and specifications: These must include a detailed description of the work to be done. A plan, drawn to scale, should be attached or referred to in the contract.

Performance: In addition, the contract should lay down conditions for suspension, arbitration, and termination (under federal law, you have three business days after signing the contract to change your mind). The contract should also provide for any changes at extra cost.

Costs and payment: The contract should outline costs, specify a payment schedule, and address the ownership of materials or structures in the event of bankruptcy.

Legal considerations: Legal provisions should include the validity period for the agreed-upon price, responsibility for permits and zoning compliance, and provisions for lien releases every time you make a payment for labor or materials (these come from the contractor and any subcontractors and material suppliers involved). Releases are necessary because even if you have paid the contractor, you can

Local Regulations

Early in the planning of your new space, consult your local building department for regulations. For many projects, from decks to fences, you will need to file for a building permit and comply with code requirements. You also need to be aware of local zoning ordinances, which can determine what and where you can build.

Code requirements vary from region to region, setting minimum safety standards for materials and construction techniques and helping to ensure that any structures you build will be safe for you and any future owners of your property.

These municipal regulations restrict the height of residential buildings, limit lot coverage, specify setbacks, and also may stipulate design standards.

In certain areas, local covenants administered by homeowners' groups have as much influence over your plans as city and county regulations. Check with your local homeowners' association for details on these restrictions.

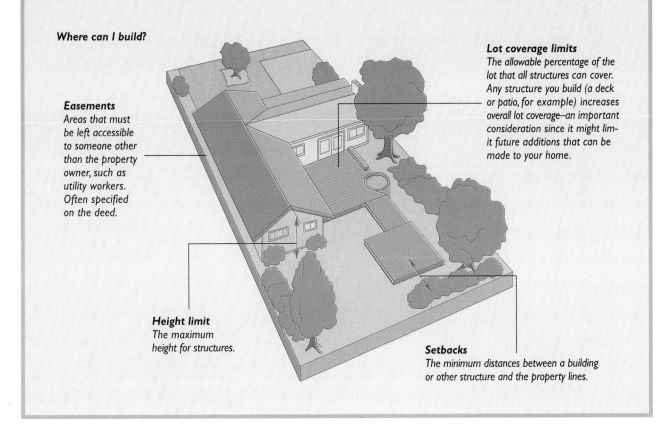

Where can I build?

Easements
Areas that must be left accessible to someone other than the property owner, such as utility workers. Often specified on the deed.

Lot coverage limits
The allowable percentage of the lot that all structures can cover. Any structure you build (a deck or patio, for example) increases overall lot coverage—an important consideration since it might limit future additions that can be made to your home.

Height limit
The maximum height for structures.

Setbacks
The minimum distances between a building or other structure and the property lines.

be held liable for any outstanding amounts owed by the contractor for the labor or for the supplies. You can also request that the builder post a bond assuring that payment will be made to all subcontractors involved.

Liability for any damages and/or personal injury incurred during the completion of the work and guarantee provisions for the contractor's work and equipment installed should also be written into a comprehensive contract.

Alternatively, you can avoid liability and protect your property before and after construction by requesting a Certificate of Insurance from your contractor. Show the certificate to your own insurance agent if you have any questions about it.

Design Ideas for a Small Lot

The backyard in the drawing below is flat and rectangular, with a concrete patio in fair condition and a wall and fencing at the perimeter of the yard. Small lots such as this one can be extremely beautiful and functional, but they pose a challenge: to create a space that suits your needs without cramming in so many features that it seems crowded.

We invited one landscape designer to create a pair of outdoor living spaces using the lot shown below as a palette. In the first example, we assumed a young couple who wanted to salvage the existing patio and provide green space and a play space for children. In the second, we assumed an older couple who enjoyed entertaining but wanted some space for quiet reflection.

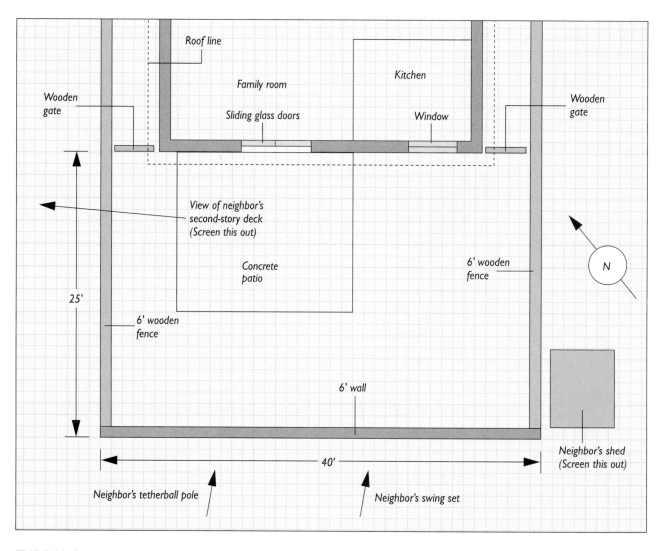

THE BASIC LOT

Not only is this lot flat and empty, but there are no special features or plants on the neighboring properties worth including visually. In fact, there are some undesirable elements: a second-story deck on the house next door, a shed abutting the back corner of the property, wooden fences at the sides that are in poor condition, and a neighbor's swing set and tetherball pole that are visible above an unattractive back wall.

Small Lot: Design 1

In this plan, the simple concrete patio is reconfigured and fragrant shrubs are planted next to the house. A concrete pathway leading to the front yard is also added. A wooden sandbox beside the patio creates a play space for young children that is easily supervised from inside or out. The location of the sandbox could instead accommodate a play house or jungle gym, depending on the youngsters' desires. A tall evergreen hedge and shade trees provide privacy and shelter, and screen out unwanted views of the fences and the neighbors' yards. Perennials and low shrubs add color to the space.
Design: Timothy N. Thoelecke Jr., APLD, ASLA, Garden Concepts, Inc.

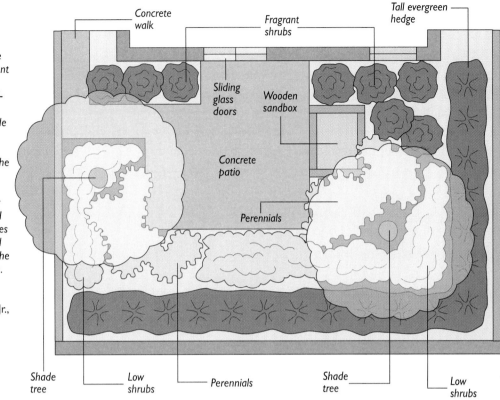

Concrete walk

Fragrant shrubs

Tall evergreen hedge

Sliding glass doors

Wooden sandbox

Concrete patio

Perennials

Shade tree

Low shrubs

Perennials

Shade tree

Low shrubs

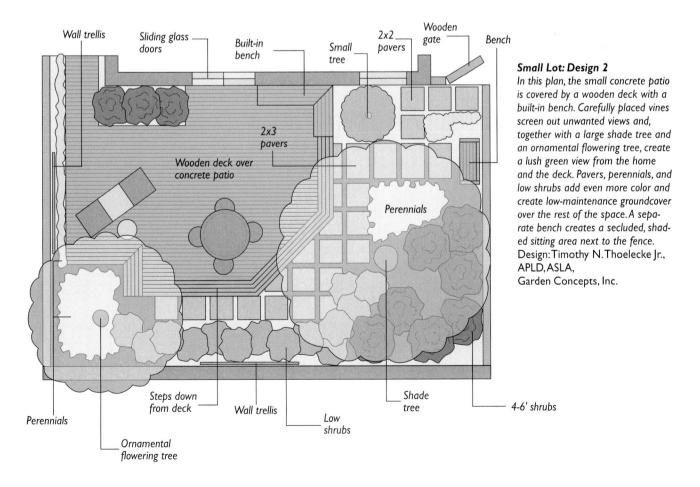

Wall trellis

Sliding glass doors

Built-in bench

Small tree

2x2 pavers

Wooden gate

Bench

2x3 pavers

Wooden deck over concrete patio

Perennials

Perennials

Steps down from deck

Wall trellis

Low shrubs

Shade tree

4-6' shrubs

Ornamental flowering tree

Small Lot: Design 2

In this plan, the small concrete patio is covered by a wooden deck with a built-in bench. Carefully placed vines screen out unwanted views and, together with a large shade tree and an ornamental flowering tree, create a lush green view from the home and the deck. Pavers, perennials, and low shrubs add even more color and create low-maintenance groundcover over the rest of the space. A separate bench creates a secluded, shaded sitting area next to the fence.
Design: Timothy N. Thoelecke Jr., APLD, ASLA, Garden Concepts, Inc.

Design Ideas for a Large Lot

As with the small-lot designs shown on the preceding pages, the plans shown on the page opposite are one landscape designer's suggestions for the sample lot below. With a larger lot, options increase.

For both designs, we assumed a middle-aged couple who like to entertain and want some relaxing green space, but who also have teenagers who enjoy sports and active play.

In this case, the lot is much larger with no existing fence surrounding it. An unappealing view of the neighbor's yard on one side of the space needs to be screened out.

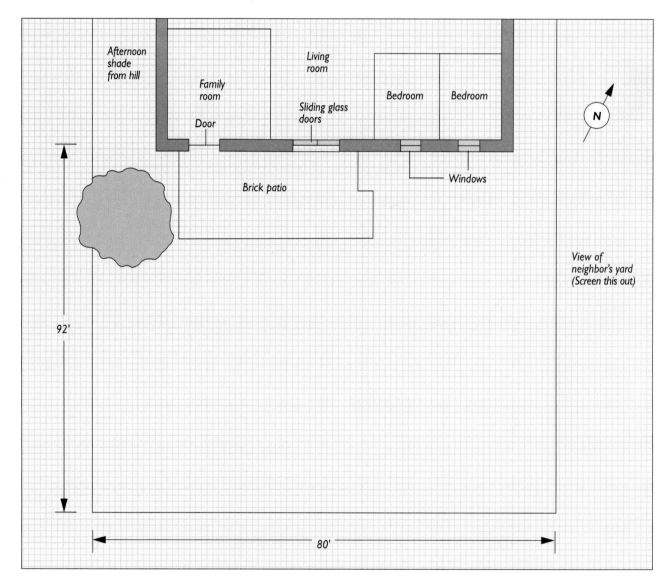

THE BASIC LOT

Bare except for a tree and a brick patio, this lot is both flat and relatively empty. Doors from the family room and living room lead into the space. Views from the two bedrooms also need to be considered.

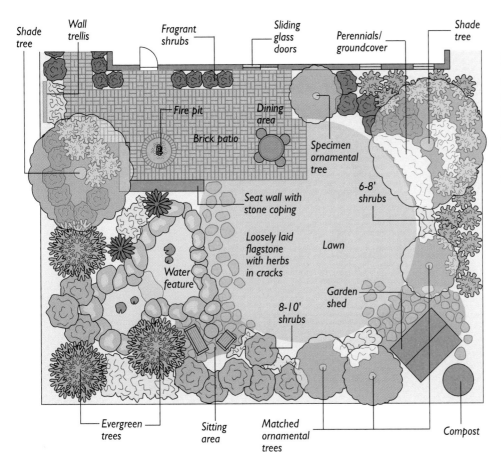

Shade tree

Wall trellis

Fragrant shrubs

Sliding glass doors

Perennials/ groundcover

Shade tree

Fire pit

Dining area

Brick patio

Specimen ornamental tree

6-8' shrubs

Seat wall with stone coping

Loosely laid flagstone with herbs in cracks

Lawn

Water feature

8-10' shrubs

Garden shed

Evergreen trees

Sitting area

Matched ornamental trees

Compost

Large Lot: Design 1

The existing brick patio is reconfigured to allow for plantings and to create a walkway leading to the front of the house. A fire pit incorporated into the patio can double as a barbecue. A seat wall with stone coping is the perfect place to watch the fire. Fragrant, colorful shrubs are planted adjacent to the house. High shrubs and a trellis along the sides and back of the property combine with evergreens, shade trees, and ornamental trees to provide color, shade, shelter, and privacy. A flagstone sitting area with herbs planted in the cracks provides a relaxing retreat next to a two-tiered pond and small waterfall. A garden shed in the corner holds tools and materials and screens out compost. A large, circular lawn provides sufficient space for games.
Design: Timothy N. Thoelecke Jr., APLD, ASLA,
Garden Concepts, Inc.

Large Lot: Design 2

In this plan, flowering shrubs and a flowering ornamental tree next to the house combine with roses to add color and fragrance to the space. The existing brick patio is reconfigured as above to allow for plantings and to create a walkway leading to the front of the house. A 6- to 8-foot hedge around the border provides shelter and privacy. Two large trees combine with a wooden overhead to provide shade. Lattice panels with windows at the back of the overhead block the wind but preserve views of the lawn from the patio. The large lawn, surrounded by brick edging and flowering shrubs, provides an open space for games. A bench serves both as a spot for watching games and as a quiet sitting area.
Design: Timothy N. Thoelecke Jr., APLD, ASLA,
Garden Concepts, Inc.

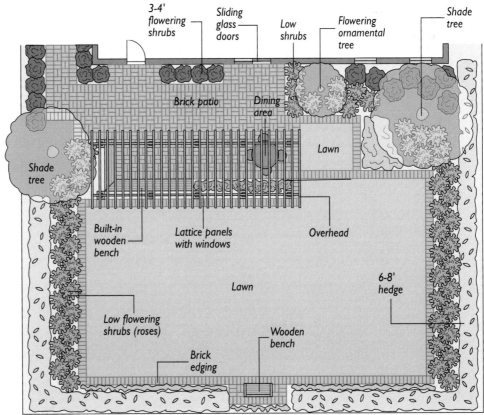

3-4' flowering shrubs

Sliding glass doors

Low shrubs

Flowering ornamental tree

Shade tree

Brick patio

Dining area

Lawn

Shade tree

Built-in wooden bench

Lattice panels with windows

Overhead

Lawn

6-8' hedge

Low flowering shrubs (roses)

Wooden bench

Brick edging

Adding
PRIVACY AND SHELTER

Privacy and shelter play a crucial role in making an outdoor living space actually livable. Providing protection from extreme weather, respite from the annoyance of bugs, and freedom from unwanted intrusions and noise, these two elements will dictate to a large degree how you feel in the space and how functional it is. And as you'll see in the following pages, the two elements truly go hand in hand. This chapter will provide you with ideas and instructions for enclosing your space and sheltering it from the weather and bugs. A few step-by-step projects— including screening in an outdoor room—will allow you to implement some changes right away.

A Secluded Retreat

Whether you're a private person or the friendliest neighbor on the block, you will want some degree of privacy and shelter in your living space. As you formulate your plan and decide on the placement of various elements in your yard, keep the following points in mind.

Privacy and shelter complement each other—as you gain in one, you invariably improve the other. A high fence, for example, not only protects from wind, it also shields you from onlookers. An awning with screens creates a sense of enclosure at the same time that it prevents you from being soaked by rain and feasted on by bugs. Think of these elements together, and try to accomplish both goals at once.

Climate will determine to a large extent your needs for shelter. Prevailing winds may need screening; extremely hot or rainy climates will definitely call for some sort of overhead structure. The information contained in Chapter 2 will offer you some guidance as you determine your needs.

When planning for privacy, consider the spots where you are likely to want a retreat from the world. This may be a small dining space for your family to eat in peace or an area for entertaining. Consider the views around the property that might impinge on your sense of seclusion in these spaces. You may want to block a clear sight line to the street or a view into a neighbor's yard. Bear in mind that you may not need to fence or wall in your entire living space to create a sense of privacy. A few judiciously placed screens can conceal the offending views and still maintain a sense of openness in the living space. As well, consider nuisance noises that you may want to be screened out, such as nearby traffic or play areas.

A high wooden fence provides an attractive form of protection from the wind and transforms this simple sitting area into a private space.

Fences, Walls, and Screens

As the old saying goes, good fences make good neighbors. Substitute walls and screens in that quotation and it is equally true. Along with trees, shrubs, and hedges (page 78), these man-made structures are among the most useful for enclosing outdoor living spaces. Apart from simply providing form to a space by defining its perimeter, these structures, depending on their height and thickness, can ensure some measure of privacy, screening out views and noise, and also function as windbreaks and climbing surfaces for vines. You can even use these structures to subdivide a large space into a series of smaller ones. This subdivision can actually make a space seem much larger because it prevents you from seeing the entire area at one time, creating a sense of mystery and surprise.

The following pages contain some excellent options for fences, walls, and screens. As a visit to your local garden center will bear out, these are just a few of the materials and design choices at your disposal. When making your choice, try to keep things simple. If you plan to construct a wall, make sure you have the skills to do so. Also temper practicality with aesthetics, choosing a structure that, while serving the needs of your family, will also reflect the style of your yard.

WIND DIRECTION/FENCE HEIGHT

Wind control studies indicate that a solid vertical screen or fence isn't necessarily the best barrier against the wind. Lattice or spaced-wood screening provides diffused protection from the wind near a fence. A fence-top baffle aimed into the wind offers the most shelter.

Solid vertical barrier
Protection drops off at a distance roughly equal to barrier's height

12'   6'

Spaced-wood screen
Wind diffused near screen, with best protection 6' to 12' from barrier

12'   6'

Solid barrier, baffle angled toward patio
Best protection up to 8' from barrier

12'   6'

Solid barrier, baffle angled into wind
Good protection near barrier and to a distance of more than twice barrier's height

12'   6'

The best way to accomplish this goal is to echo in the structure some color or architectural element of your home or of the rest of the living space. This is often a simple matter of painting the fence, screen, or wall a color matching that of the trim on your home. If your home or patio is brick, however, it may mean constructing a brick wall. Your choice of material will also be governed by what is in the rest of the space. A natural, informal garden area filled with natural materials will be best complemented by a natural wall.

FENCES

Wooden fences are ideal for containing an area, as well as tempering wind and noise. They also can be attractive additions to a space. However, they are less stable than walls and require periodic painting and replacing of damaged boards.

Fences are often the best solution to a variety of issues you may have concerning your outdoor living space. First and foremost, fences deter unwanted entry. If that is your main concern, choose a solid-board or panel design—

they are the most effective deterrents—and plan to install a secure lock on any gate.

As shown by the small selection below, there is a wide variety of wooden fence types. Many more styles are available in materials from iron to aluminum. To extend the life of a wooden fence, use a naturally decay-resistant wood or pressure-treated lumber. Wood posts set in soil should be treated with preservative rated for soil exposure. Check local codes for restrictions before building a fence.

A SELECTION OF WOOD FENCES

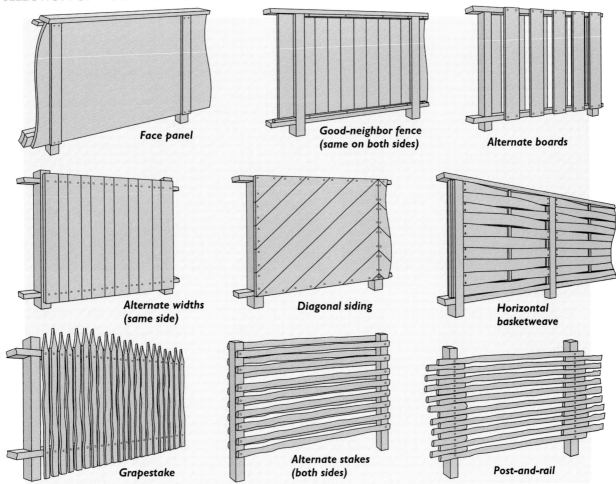

Face panel

Good-neighbor fence (same on both sides)

Alternate boards

Alternate widths (same side)

Diagonal siding

Horizontal basketweave

Grapestake

Alternate stakes (both sides)

Post-and-rail

FENCE CONSTRUCTION

Fence building has three basic stages: setting and aligning the posts, fastening the rails, and attaching the siding. These procedures are shown below for a simple board fence on level ground.

To begin, plot the course of your fence, and use stakes and string to mark the location of the end and corner posts. Know where your property lines are so you can be sure the fence is on your land. **Setting and aligning the posts:** This step is best done by two people—one to hold and align the post while the other fills the hole with concrete or tamped soil. For the fence to be solid, it's essential that your posts are secure and stable. Posts should be spaced evenly; for wood fences posts are normally spaced at 7- to 8-foot intervals. For greatest stability, posts should be of a length so that one half their exposed height is underground. For residential fencing between 3 and 6 feet tall, set posts a minimum of 2 feet deep. Each posthole's diameter should be two to three times larger than the post's width or diameter.

Add gravel for drainage, then backfill the holes with the posts in place. Soil backfill is adequate for light fences—such as lath, picket, and some post-and-board types—or for fences up to 4 feet in height. In unstable ground, use concrete *(below, Step 1)*. For a fence that will not undergo much horizontal stress (such as heavy snow loads in winter), a good compromise is to set the corner and end posts in

Building a simple fence

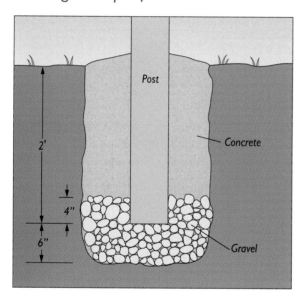

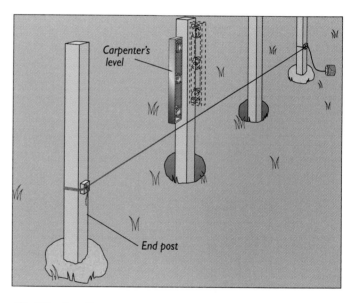

1 Setting the posts
Starting with a corner or end post, set the post into the hole in a bed of 4 to 6 inches of gravel for drainage. Mix concrete and shovel it in evenly around the post. Work a scrap board up and down in the concrete to release any air pockets. Using a carpenter's level, check that the post is plumb. Continue filling until the concrete extends 1 to 2 inches above ground level. With a mason's trowel, slope the top away from the post to divert water *(above)*. Plumb the post again. Allow the concrete to cure for two days before attaching rails and siding.

2 Aligning the posts
For short sections of fence, use a carpenter's level and string to align the posts. Start by setting and plumbing the two end posts so their faces are parallel. Then, cut 2-inch-long 1x2 spacer blocks and tack them to the posts about 2 feet above the ground. Stretch twine between the posts, wrapping it over the spacer blocks. (The blocks will keep the intermediate posts from touching the string and throwing it out of alignment.) Set and align the intermediate posts at a distance away from the string that is equal to the thickness of the spacers. Plumb each post on two faces *(above)* as you backfill the holes with soil and tamp with a 2x4.

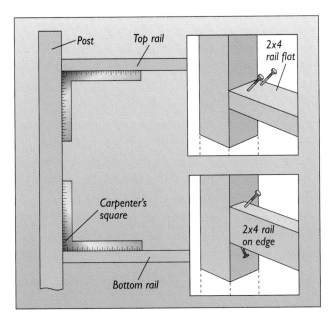

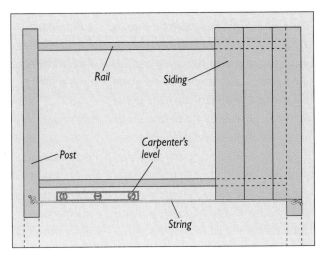

3 Attaching rails

With someone helping to hold the rail level, position it between the posts so its edges are flush with the posts' front and back faces *(inset, top)*; use a carpenter's square to make sure the rail is perpendicular to the posts *(above)*. Then, drive the nails into the posts. For fences with long sections of heavy siding, place the rails on edge *(inset, bottom)* to help prevent the fence from sagging under its own weight. In this case, drive nails through the top and bottom of the rails.

4 Attaching siding

To keep the siding at an even height along the fence line, make sure all the pieces are cut to the same length. Stretch and level a string from post to post at the height above the ground where you want the bottom of the siding. Position the first board and check it for plumb. Then, butt each of the following boards against the one before it *(above)*. Periodically check the vertical alignment of the boards with a carpenter's level and be sure to keep the bottoms of the boards aligned with the string. Fasten the boards to the rails with galvanized nails three times as long as the thickness of the siding.

concrete, and backfill the other posts with tamped soil.

The method of setting and aligning posts that is shown on the page opposite is best suited to short fences. Keep in mind that posts set in concrete can be adjusted for up to 20 minutes after the concrete has been cast; after that, they should not be moved.

Fastening rails: No matter what type of fence you'll be building, there are a limited number of ways to attach rails to posts. Because the joints between rails and posts will trap moisture, you should first apply a finish or preservative as protection against decay to all surfaces where the rails and posts come into contact. This is recommended even if the wood you're using for rails is pressure-treated or naturally decay-resistant. For fences with 4x4 posts and 2x4 rails to which wooden siding will be attached, rails should be cut to fit snugly between the posts, then toenailed in place with 3-inch galvanized nails to avoid rust lines on your fence. To start the nails, lay each rail on the ground and drive the nails in partway. Then, with a helper holding a rail level at one end, position the rail between the posts so the rail edges are flush with the front and back faces of the posts; use a carpenter's square to make certain each rail is perpendicular to the posts. Then, use a hammer to drive the nails into the posts.

Attaching siding: How you attach the siding will depend on the material you're using and on your fence design. The illustration in Step 4 above shows a typical board fence, simple siding to attach. See page 37 for other fence designs.

SCREENS

The visual appeal of screens makes them an excellent alternative to fences and walls. Screens can be used practically anywhere in your living space to shield you from noise and wind as well as divide areas and block out undesirable views.

Lattice screens are an ideal way to provide shelter without blocking out balmy breezes. They are also excellent structures for supporting climbing plants, which provide additional privacy. A word of caution:

lattice is a strong visual element. It will stick out like a sore thumb unless there are other lattice features nearby.

Lattice is inexpensive and does not require any special expertise to install. Most lumberyards and home building centers carry 4- by 8-foot prefabricated lattice panels, a simpler, less expensive option than making them yourself. Be sure to inspect the panels for cracks, splintering, and loose staples. Unless

the panels are cedar or another naturally decay-resistant wood, be sure that they have been pressure-treated. Cheaply made panels will need to be replaced regularly. Maintenance-free polyvinylchloride (PVC) lattice is also available.

Below are a selection of attractive screens suitable for outdoor living spaces, including a transparent unit with acrylic or glass that is perfect for screening out wind and noise while preserving views.

SCREEN POSSIBILITIES

The function of a screen is primarily as a visual or climatic barrier. The drawings below illustrate some popular screen patterns.

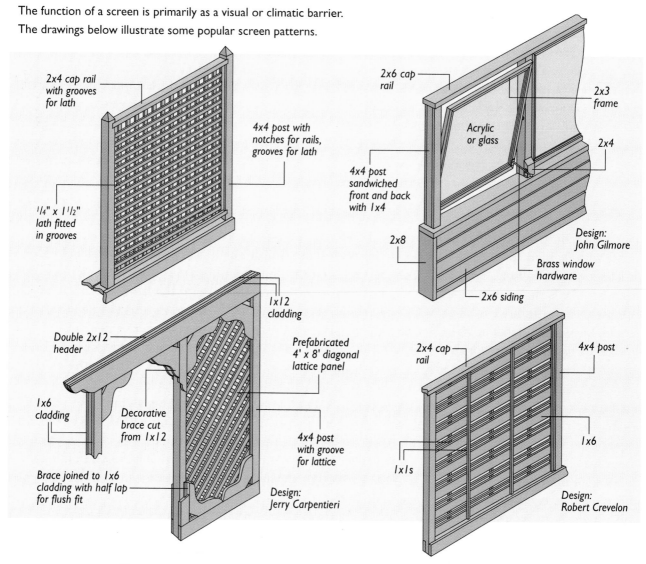

2x4 cap rail with grooves for lath

4x4 post with notches for rails, grooves for lath

$1/4$" x $1 1/2$" lath fitted in grooves

2x6 cap rail

2x3 frame

Acrylic or glass

2x4

4x4 post sandwiched front and back with 1x4

2x8

Design: John Gilmore

Brass window hardware

2x6 siding

Double 2x12 header

1x12 cladding

1x6 cladding

Decorative brace cut from 1x12

Prefabricated 4' x 8' diagonal lattice panel

4x4 post with groove for lattice

Brace joined to 1x6 cladding with half lap for flush fit

Design: Jerry Carpentieri

2x4 cap rail

4x4 post

1x6

1x1s

Design: Robert Crevelon

Masonry walls—those made from concrete, brick, stone, or adobe—are you best choice when you want a wall that will last a lifetime.

Brick and stone are two of the most attractive options. Both are examples of what is called unit masonry—materials small enough for one person to handle. Brick and stone are available in a wide range of styles, colors, and textures. The best stone to use is often that which can be found locally and will blend into the surroundings. Stone that has been transported long distances will cost more and may look out of place. Stone comes either rough-hewn or dressed. Rough stones are used in dry stone walls (no mortar). Dressed, or shaped, stone has a more uniform surface and is better suited to formal settings. If you opt for stone or brick, be sure it matches any brick or stone used on the home's exterior.

Adobe is the southwest's version of the mud brick. With its warm, earthy color, it creates a friendly, informal tone. It is found only in New Mexico, so delivery charges outside the west make it an expensive choice.

Finally, concrete, either cast or in block form, can be a handsome wall material. Blocks come in many sizes and textures. They are cheaper to purchase and easier to install than bricks and can be painted to match the color of your home.

Selection of the site is important to a wall's longevity. Choose a place where the drainage is good and the soil is firm. If the wall is near the root systems of large trees you'll need to use a gravel or tamped-soil foundation and dry stack the wall, so roots won't trouble it.

Unless you are experienced in working with concrete or building masonry walls, it is a good idea to leave this work to a professional contractor. Dry stone walls are the easiest to build.

Stacked rough stones create a natural-looking informal garden wall—worthy of the time and effort involved in selecting just the right stone for the right spot.

Overheads

Overheads are a great way to provide shade, add privacy, create leafy canopies and tunnels, and generally add variety and interest to a living space. Overheads also function as "space frames" that can define all or part of your outdoor living area.

When you are deciding where to place your overhead, consider spots where you will be sitting in full sun for hours at a time as well as eating and entertaining areas.

Consider also the style of your home and choose roofing material that will complement it. Below you will find a selection of overhead roofing materials. Open materials provide a light, airy feel; closed provide more shelter. Your overhead may be freestanding *(page opposite)* or attached to the house with a ledger *(page 46)*. Screening can be attached to an overhead framework as part of a screened room,

although many screened-in areas have roofs like a house *(page 50)*.

If an overhead seems too permanent, there are plenty of temporary alternatives. Commercial awnings, tents, and canopies (such as the one shown on the page opposite) are available in a vast array of styles and can be set up for specific seasons and then removed and stored. Some models include attachable screening panels to ward off bugs.

A GALLERY OF OVERHEAD COVERS

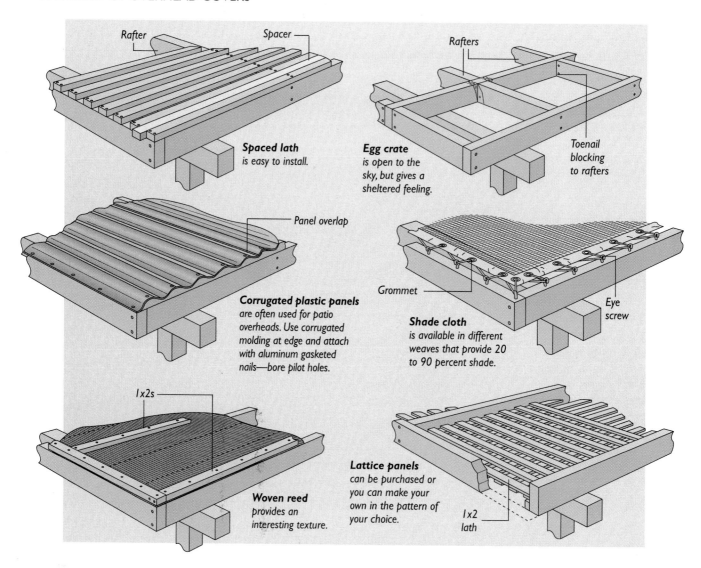

Rafter · Spacer

Spaced lath is easy to install.

Rafters

Toenail blocking to rafters

Egg crate is open to the sky, but gives a sheltered feeling.

Panel overlap

Corrugated plastic panels are often used for patio overheads. Use corrugated molding at edge and attach with aluminum gasketed nails—bore pilot holes.

Grommet

Eye screw

Shade cloth is available in different weaves that provide 20 to 90 percent shade.

1x2s

Woven reed provides an interesting texture.

Lattice panels can be purchased or you can make your own in the pattern of your choice.

1x2 lath

Coordinated colors of the canopy, house, and outdoor furniture create a seamless link between home and patio.

Sunlight brightens this outdoor spot without disturbing diners, thanks to a handsome overhead. The structure also emphasizes the canopy effect of the surrounding trees.

BUILDING A BASIC OVERHEAD

The steps below will give you a general idea of the building sequence for a freestanding overhead. Sizes, spans, and spacings of framing materials must meet local code requirements. In areas with harsh winters, your structure will have to support the weight of snow and ice.

The main components of an overhead are posts, beams, rafters, and surfacing. When an overhead is attached to the house, a ledger takes the place of one beam *(page 46)*. Roofing can take many forms.

Special connectors and fasteners strengthen the structure and make building easier. Post anchors hold posts in place. They can be set in a concrete slab just after the concrete has been placed. Post anchors can also be fastened to an existing slab with lag screws and anchor shields or to piers set outside the patio perimeter *(page opposite)*.

Assembling an overhead frame

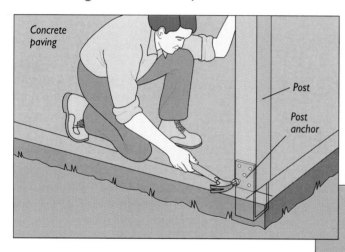

Concrete paving

Post

Post anchor

1 Setting the posts
Cut posts to length and nail post/beam connectors on top. Place the posts in post anchors. Keep the posts vertical and nail the post anchors to them *(left)*. (The post anchors shown must be used with a new concrete slab.)

2 Plumbing the posts
Plumb each post using a carpenter's level placed on two adjacent sides. Secure the posts in position with temporary wooden braces nailed to stakes driven into the ground *(right)*.

Level

Temporary wooden brace

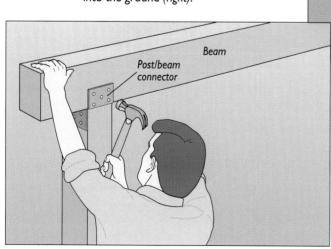

Beam

Post/beam connector

3 Attach beams and rafters
Position a beam on top of the posts that will support it. Check that the posts are vertical and the beam is level, and make adjustments as necessary. Nail the post/beam connectors to the beam *(left)*. Set and space rafters on the tops of the beams and secure them with framing anchors.

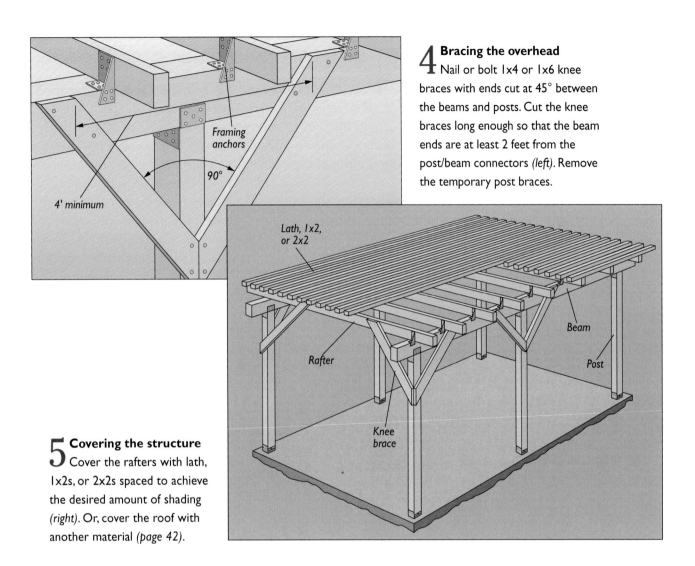

4 Bracing the overhead
Nail or bolt 1x4 or 1x6 knee braces with ends cut at 45° between the beams and posts. Cut the knee braces long enough so that the beam ends are at least 2 feet from the post/beam connectors *(left)*. Remove the temporary post braces.

Framing anchors

90°

4' minimum

Lath, 1x2, or 2x2

Beam

Rafter

Post

Knee brace

5 Covering the structure
Cover the rafters with lath, 1x2s, or 2x2s spaced to achieve the desired amount of shading *(right)*. Or, cover the roof with another material *(page 42)*.

Post Anchor Options

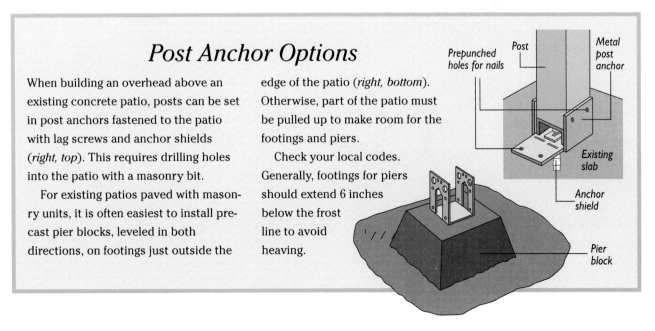

When building an overhead above an existing concrete patio, posts can be set in post anchors fastened to the patio with lag screws and anchor shields *(right, top)*. This requires drilling holes into the patio with a masonry bit.

For existing patios paved with masonry units, it is often easiest to install precast pier blocks, leveled in both directions, on footings just outside the edge of the patio *(right, bottom)*. Otherwise, part of the patio must be pulled up to make room for the footings and piers.

Check your local codes. Generally, footings for piers should extend 6 inches below the frost line to avoid heaving.

Prepunched holes for nails

Post

Metal post anchor

Existing slab

Anchor shield

Pier block

LEDGER

Some overheads rely on the use of a ledger to support one end of the rafters at the house. If your overhead will serve as a roof for a screened room connected to your home, it should be supported by a ledger. The ledger must be fastened to a masonry wall or to the framing of a wood-frame house. If you have a one-story house, you'll fasten the ledger to wall studs; or, if the overhead falls just under the house roof, you can attach the ledger to the rafters. On a two-story house, you can attach the ledger to the floor framing as shown below. Locate the middle of the ledger about 6 inches below the interior floor level. To transfer this measurement to the exterior wall, use a window or door sill as a reference point.

Securing the ledger: First you'll need to brace or nail the ledger temporarily at the desired height; make sure it's perfectly level. For a wood-frame house, drill lag-screw holes into the framing every 16 inches as shown and screw the ledger in place with ⅜-inch lag screws and flat washers. For a masonry wall, use anchor shields, lag screws, and washers at the same intervals.

Keeping the rain at bay: Unless the ledger is protected from the rain by the eaves or by its own solid cover material and flashing, you'll have to prevent water from accumulating in the joint between the ledger and the house. To do this, space the ledger out from the wall with flat washers. Or, you can protect the ledger with aluminum or galvanized sheet-metal Z-flashing.

ATTACHING A LEDGER TO A TWO-STORY HOUSE

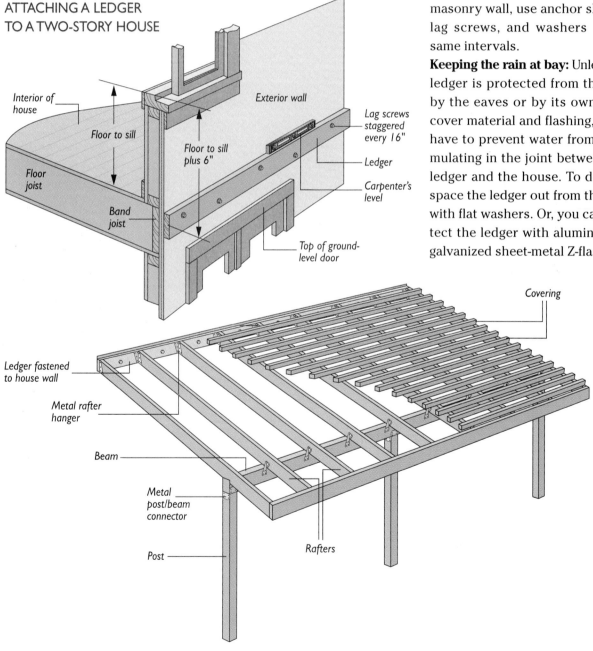

Interior of house

Floor to sill

Floor joist

Band joist

Floor to sill plus 6"

Exterior wall

Lag screws staggered every 16"

Ledger

Carpenter's level

Top of ground-level door

Covering

Ledger fastened to house wall

Metal rafter hanger

Beam

Metal post/beam connector

Post

Rafters

Screened Rooms

In some regions, enjoyment of outdoor living spaces is limited greatly by bugs. The evening hours, when mosquitoes come to life, can be downright unbearable unless some form of protection is in place. The easiest way to keep bugs at bay is to enclose a part of your space with screens.

If you're starting from scratch, installing a commercial awning or canopy with screens is probably the easiest and quickest route to a full-fledged screened room. Many manufacturers market screening attachments for their overheads, installed by one of several simple methods—spline systems and spe-

cial screen-holding tape are just a couple of ways—that create an attractive screened space in little time and at reasonable cost. These screens usually have the added benefit that they are relatively easy to remove.

If you have a patio roof or overhead above your porch, deck, or

Screening in a space doesn't necessarily mean creating an imposing sense of enclosure. With its high screened walls, this small outdoor room maintains an open feel.

A screened room allows diners to enjoy the evening breeze and views of the yard safe from bugs. Blinds on the south wall can be opened to shelter the space from sunlight when necessary.

patio, adding screens is a fairly straightforward task. The easiest method involves installing 1x1 stops on the support members of the overhead structure and stapling screening to it. The staples and screening edges are then covered with a special molding called screen bead. The one problem with this approach is that the screens will not be removable. A second approach, shown in steps starting on page 50, involves mounting screened frames in the openings. This requires more time and effort, but the structure will be much sturdier and the screens can be removed and stored if necessary in winter. For both methods, use pressure-treated lumber for sole plates laid on the deck, porch, or patio surface.

Whatever method you choose, remember that bugs can slip through the smallest of openings.

The covering on an overhead used for a screened room will have to be impervious to bugs. Also, if you have clapboard or shingle siding, you may need to caulk gaps between the house wall and the screen framing.

The only other decision you need to make is about the screening to use. See the sidebar on the page opposite for information on different screening materials.

Screening Options

Screening has evolved a great deal over the past 100 years. Originally fashioned from horse hair, today this invaluable material in the battle against bugs is most commonly made of aluminum or vinyl-coated fiberglass. In terms of performance, there is little to differentiate these two types of screening material. Both are rustproof and stain-resistant. The major difference is how they react when contacted: aluminum tends to dent easily whereas vinyl-coated fiberglass stretches and may tear.

Aluminum comes in black, dark gray, and bright aluminum colors, and costs about 35 cents per square foot. When choosing screening, bear in mind that darker colors are most opaque from outside, but offer the best visibility from inside. Aluminum is available in 18x16 mesh, which simply means that in every square inch there are 18 horizontal and 16 vertical wires, each .011 mil in size. It is sold in 7-, 25-, and 100-foot rolls in widths ranging from 18 to 72 inches.

Vinyl-coated fiberglass is the least expensive and best-selling type of screening. It comes in three colors: aquamarine, silver-gray, and dark gray. Fiberglass screening for screened rooms often has larger wires—.013 mil—for greater strength and a more open mesh—18x14 rather than 18x16. An ultra-fine 20x20 mesh is also available. It keeps out even the tiniest of insects, but won't allow much breeze through either. Solar screening is also made from vinyl-coated fiber-glass. It is a dense mesh that shades most sunlight but allows good visi-bility from inside. By reducing ultra-violet radiation, solar screening also helps preserve the color of outdoor furniture. All vinyl-coated fiberglass screening comes in roughly the same size rolls as aluminum and at a slightly lower cost.

Other screen materials include bronze, copper, brass, and stainless steel. These are more costly, though, ranging from $1 to more than $2 per square foot.

Clay-tile roofing and aluminum screen frames give this outdoor room quite a different look from its traditional wood-framed cousins. Dark screening material offers some privacy by preventing a clear view into the space from outside.

ANATOMY OF A SCREENED ROOM

With a roof already in place, openings are framed by 4x4 posts and 2x4 studs, sole plates, top plates, knee rails, and knee-rail supports. Screen surrounds consist of 2x4 frames and 2x2 stops; removable screen frames fashioned from 1x4s are screwed to the stops. The doorway king studs, jack studs, and header are positioned to accommodate a prefabricated screen door.

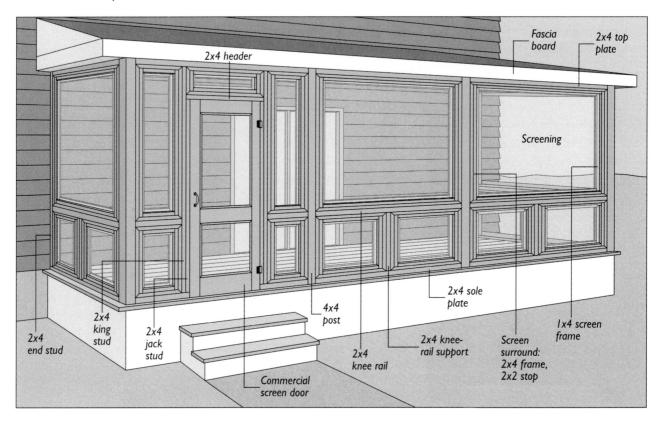

Fascia board

2x4 top plate

2x4 header

Screening

2x4 sole plate

4x4 post

1x4 screen frame

2x4 end stud

2x4 king stud

2x4 jack stud

2x4 knee-rail support

Screen surround: 2x4 frame, 2x2 stop

2x4 knee rail

Commercial screen door

Screening in a deck or porch

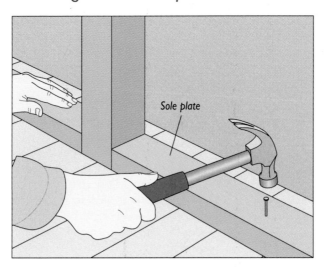

Sole plate

1 Attaching sole and top plates
Sole and top plates are 2x4 horizontal supports placed between the bottoms and tops of the posts that support your overhead or porch roof. Cut them to length and nail or screw them to the ceiling and floor every 16 inches, if possible to joists *(left)*. Leave an opening for a doorway 3¼ inches wider than the commercial screen door you plan to use. If the floor surface is concrete or brick, you will have to shim sole plates and fasten them with anchor shields and lag screws (see sidebar page 52). Once the sole and top plates are installed, frame the door opening as shown above.

2 Installing knee rails

Cut 2x4 knee rails to fit between the posts. Cut a pair of 2x4 knee-rail supports to hold up the ends of each board, then toenail the knee rails in place about 3 feet above the sole plates *(right)*. If the distances between posts are long, fasten extra knee-rail supports midway between posts.

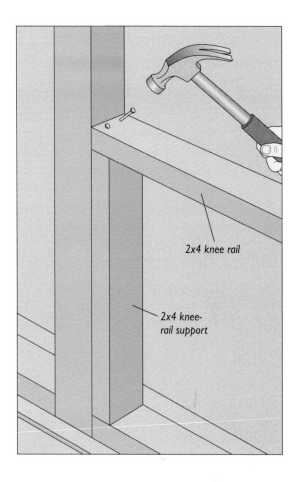

2x4 knee rail

2x4 knee-rail support

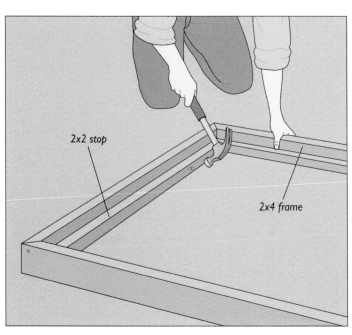

2x2 stop

2x4 frame

3 Building screen surrounds

Assemble frames of beveled 2x4s to fit in the openings formed by the support members. Attach 2x2 stops flush with the outside edge of the frames *(above)*.

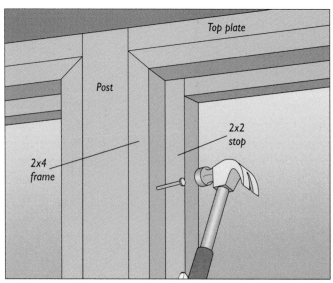

Top plate

Post

2x4 frame

2x2 stop

4 Installing the screen surrounds

Nail the screen surrounds into place in the openings *(right)*. Check the corners for square as you go and adjust the surrounds if necessary.

5 Making the screen frames

Measure the openings of the screen surrounds carefully, then assemble 1x4 screen frames to fit the openings. Join the frames at the corners with L-brackets. Next, cut pieces of screening slighting larger than the frame openings. Pull the screening taut *(right)* and fasten it to the screen frames with rustproof staples every 2 inches. Trim excess screening material with scissors or a utility knife.

1x4 screen frame

1x4 screen frame

6 Securing the frames in place

Secure the frames to the stops on the surrounds with screws *(left)*. This will allow you to remove the screens easily for repair or storage.

Screening in a Patio

For proper drainage, well-built patios slope away from the house slightly. If you are screening in a patio, you will need to compensate for this slope by shimming the sole plates that run away from the house so they are perfectly level. Insert the shims to support the sole plate and check for level *(right)*. Trim the shims flush with the edges of the sole plates.

On a concrete or brick patio, you will also have to use a different method to fasten the sole plates. Mark the location of the sole plates on the patio, then drill holes every 18 inches for anchor shields, leaving an opening for a doorway. Shim the sole plates, then fasten them by driving lag screws through them into the anchor shields. Seal gaps with caulk.

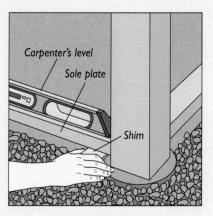

Carpenter's level

Sole plate

Shim

Gazebos

Gazebos have been used as shelters as far back as the Renaissance. Traditionally they were small shelters located specifically to take advantage of a particular view. In the modern living space, gazebos are often used simply as garden retreats or even as outdoor dining areas. No matter, since a gazebo provides such a strong focal point in your outdoor living space, you should pay careful attention to its placement as well as to its design. To determine the placement and size of your gazebo, refer to your base plan. Move a scale cutout of the gazebo base to various positions. If the gazebo is far off in a corner of your living space it can serve as a quiet retreat, but make sure it isn't so far away that you won't use it often. If you position it in the center of your garden, it will act as a focal point of the living space. The design should mirror or complement your house's architecture and fit the style of the living space it will inhabit.

Today gazebos come in a wide range of styles, from traditional, wooden, open-sided hexagonal and octagonal models to more modern units made of steel and glass.

Building a gazebo requires great patience and painstaking computing of angles and joints. Better options are to have one built by a contractor modeled after a design you like or to purchase a prefabricated kit, available at many home building centers. Check the type and quality of wood used and whether it needs a protective finish applied to it before assembly. Also ask about a warranty. Most kits will go up in a few short hours.

Traditionally gazebos were built as viewing pavilions. Located at a distance from the home adjacent to a sparkling pond, this one also serves as a spot for quiet reflection.

Bringing the INDOORS OUT

With the right design, furniture, and other amenities, patio and garden spaces can stand in for almost any room in the house, allowing you to enjoy the outdoors to its fullest as you cook, entertain, or simply relax in the privacy of your backyard. The following chapter contains a full menu of ideas and a few easy-to-build projects for your outdoor room. Sections on outdoor kitchens, dining areas, relaxation areas, and furniture contain dozens of suggestions to inspire you and some commonsense tips to ensure your installations fit your needs. Finally, we help you tackle the challenges of outdoor lighting and heating by presenting a variety of options and techniques as well as information on installing a low-voltage lighting system, all of which will help you enjoy your garden and patio living spaces well into the night.

Outdoor Kitchens

For many homeowners, cooking outdoors is one of summer's great pleasures. While creating an outdoor kitchen can be as simple as setting up a portable barbecue or hibachi next to a picnic table, it can also involve much more.

If you're a dedicated outdoor chef with enough space—especially if you live in a climate that allows year-round outdoor cooking—you may want to plan a more elaborate and permanent outdoor kitchen.

In addition to built-in cooking facilities, other amenities include preparation and serving counters, storage cabinets (for cooking mitts and various barbecue utensils), and perhaps a refrigerator and a sink. A great advantage of these permanent installations over portable barbecues is that they usually run on piped-in natural gas rather than containers of propane or charcoal (both of which can run out at inconvenient moments).

LAYOUT AND DESIGN

In colder, windier climates, your outdoor kitchen—like the nearby dining area—should have good protection from the wind and sun. Your site should take advantage of existing protection, such as the side of the house or wall of the garage, potting shed, or corner where a wing meets the main house. Fences *(page 36)* or natural wind screens like hedges *(page 78)* can reduce the influence of prevailing winds and provide late-afternoon shade. In warm climates,

open the area to breezes to help ensure cooler temperatures. For more on weather, see page 21.

Remember that no matter how well-appointed your kitchen is, some of the food cooked outside will be prepared or stored inside and the leftovers will be returned there later. With this in mind, outdoor kitchens should be accessible to the indoor kitchen. Smooth, well-tended paths leading from the house are crucial for shuttling back and forth (a serving cart will also make this much easier and convenient). Use the base plan you created to place your kitchen as well as dining and other outdoor living areas in the best location.

To help keep outdoor cooking facilities clean, choose materials carefully. Glazed ceramic tiles, for example, are an excellent choice for countertops. Wood, on the other hand, should be avoided. Materials used for counters, fireplaces, or fire pits should also complement house and patio building materials. For example, if you plan to build with bricks, they should match the bricks used in walls or paving.

OUTDOOR BARBECUES

Barbecues range from basic units to more elaborate models like the high-tech version shown on page 56. Several mid-range models used as part of a permanent outdoor

With a sink, refrigerator, and ample cupboard space, this outdoor kitchen has all the amenities of its indoor counterpart. Installations such as this one should be protected under an overhang or overhead.

kitchen design are shown opposite. Your choice will depend on factors such as the number of people you'll be serving and the kinds of food you'll be preparing. Outdoor cooking need not be limited to hamburgers and steaks. With options like built-in grills, ovens, and smokers, you can prepare dishes ranging from smoked salmon to stir-fried vegetables to fresh bread.

The most popular charcoal-fired barbecues are open braziers, covered kettles, and boxed units with lids. Open braziers vary from table-top portables to large freestanding models. Covered kettles and boxes with hinged lids can be used covered or open for cooking with direct or indirect heat.

Most gas and some electrical models use a briquet-shaped mate-

rial such as lava rock above the burner. Features such as smokers, auxiliary burners, and rotisseries allow extra flexibility. Smokers, for example, can merely add smoke flavoring to grilled food or can be designed to "cold-smoke" food. Barbecues with the same capabilities as gas ranges allow you to prepare sauces and other dishes outside. Rotisseries allow the slow

THE WELL-EQUIPPED GRILL

The defining feature of a barbecue is its grill, suspended above a burning source of heat. But some modern barbecues can do more than just grill—their various features can often rival an indoor range top. The barbecue at right has the elements for virtually any approach to cooking.

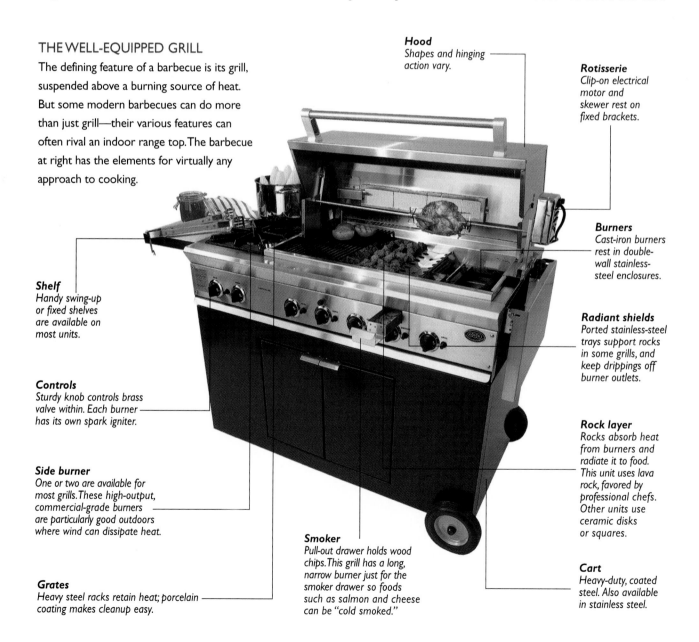

Hood
Shapes and hinging action vary.

Rotisserie
Clip-on electrical motor and skewer rest on fixed brackets.

Burners
Cast-iron burners rest in double-wall stainless-steel enclosures.

Radiant shields
Ported stainless-steel trays support rocks in some grills, and keep drippings off burner outlets.

Rock layer
Rocks absorb heat from burners and radiate it to food. This unit uses lava rock, favored by professional chefs. Other units use ceramic disks or squares.

Cart
Heavy-duty, coated steel. Also available in stainless steel.

Shelf
Handy swing-up or fixed shelves are available on most units.

Controls
Sturdy knob controls brass valve within. Each burner has its own spark igniter.

Side burner
One or two are available for most grills. These high-output, commercial-grade burners are particularly good outdoors where wind can dissipate heat.

Grates
Heavy steel racks retain heat; porcelain coating makes cleanup easy.

Smoker
Pull-out drawer holds wood chips. This grill has a long, narrow burner just for the smoker drawer so foods such as salmon and cheese can be "cold smoked."

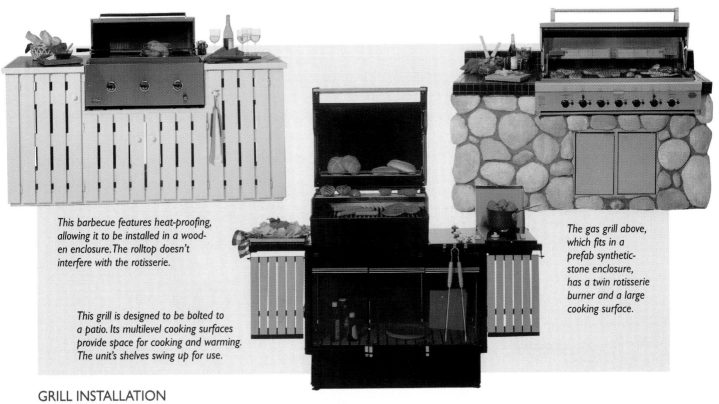

This barbecue features heat-proofing, allowing it to be installed in a wooden enclosure. The rolltop doesn't interfere with the rotisserie.

This grill is designed to be bolted to a patio. Its multilevel cooking surfaces provide space for cooking and warming. The unit's shelves swing up for use.

The gas grill above, which fits in a prefab synthetic-stone enclosure, has a twin rotisserie burner and a large cooking surface.

GRILL INSTALLATION

When selecting outdoor cooking facilities, think carefully about the types of food you like to cook as well as the number of people you'll be cooking for and choose a unit that will accommodate your needs. The barbecue models shown above are designed for permanent outdoor kitchen installation and offer a range of cooking and design variations. They are also less expensive than the full-feature model shown opposite.

roasting of larger cuts of meat. Instant-on grills and other built-in conveniences make the barbecue as easy to use as a kitchen range.

UTILITIES

To install an outdoor kitchen, an electrical cable or conduit will likely need to be routed to the site underground or, if the kitchen is next to the house, via an exterior wall or overhead. In cold climates water pipes must be set below the frost line; drainpipes must be sloped toward the main drain. Natural gas lines must be buried 12 to 18 inches underground (gas will flow even in cold temperatures).

Outdoor electrical outlets must be protected by watertight boxes and a ground-fault circuit interrupter (GFCI), which shuts off power to the circuit in the event of a short. For more on wiring the outdoors, see page 73.

If you're planning an extensive kitchen addition outside, it's best to consult a landscape architect or contractor who specializes in the kind of additions you'll need.

FIREPLACES AND FIRE PITS

Outdoor fireplaces and fire pits are less versatile than full-feature barbecues, but they can be an attractive addition to your property,

providing the same charm—and heating—as a camp fire. For more on how a fire pit can heat your space, see the sidebar on page 59.

If your house is rustic, opt for a fire pit or a simple fireplace. Avoid designs that will dominate your garden. A tall unit may look at home among high trees, but will be out of place among low plantings. Also bear in mind that the unit will be used infrequently and should not be the focal point of the overall area.

Fireplaces and fire pits are most often masonry installations, made with concrete, brick, or stone. They range from very simple units that seem little more than a hole in the ground to ornate units that appear large enough to live in. Homeowners highly skilled in masonry work may be able to build these units themselves. The vast majority would be better off having the unit constructed by a contractor who specializes in these types of installations. Two attractive examples are shown below. Before planning for a fireplace or fire pit, check with your local building codes or consult your fire marshall about restrictions on such installations.

A fire pit brings the charm of a camp fire into a backyard setting (local regulations permitting). The addition of a grill creates basic barbecue facilities.

A stately outdoor fireplace encloses one side of a patio and serves as a beautiful design feature. A low wall further defines the area and doubles as seating space.

To get the most possible use out of your outdoor living space, you may want to consider adding some type of heating device to take the edge off the cold.

Fire pits, such as the model shown on the page opposite, are good sources of heat. Low, round metal braziers are an inexpensive and convenient option that allows you to move the heat to various locations on the patio.

Portable pottery fire pits generate large amounts of heat from a small fire. Use them cautiously: they're light and fairly fragile, and they may break if the fire inside is too hot. You'll get the best results from burning kindling-size wood.

Remember that any open fire is a potential hazard. Be sure your fire is well away from anything that could be ignited by flying sparks. In some places, a permit is needed for any outdoor fire. Call your fire department beforehand and ask about local regulations.

If a fireplace or a fire pit is not feasible, another option to consider is a patio heater. Freestanding heaters *(right)* and mounted units *(below)* are both available at home building stores and garden supply centers.

For heating units to perform well, they need to be in the right location. Pick an intimate spot. The ideal location has a combination of walls, fences, and overhead structures that will prevent the wind from blowing through your selected area and counteracting the warmth.

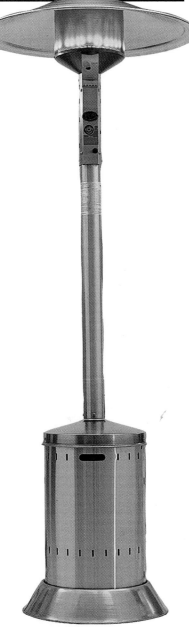

Mushroom heater
With its base hiding a propane tank, this stainless-steel heater, also known as a mushroom heater, provides a comfort zone 12 to 15 feet in diameter. Mushroom heaters are the most powerful outdoor heaters in terms of energy output, but some of the heat radiates vertically above the desired area. They must be put away when not in use since bugs, moisture, chlorine, and salt air can affect their performance.

Gas heaters
Gas-fired directional heaters mount to a house's eaves, allowing them to throw their heat efficiently without being obtrusive. They're usually quite expensive, ranging from $500 to $700 for the complete installation and hookup of two heaters. And you'll need to check them periodically for bugs and other maintenance considerations.

Dining Areas

An outdoor dining area is often the centerpiece of an attractive patio or garden environment, and can double as a sewing spot or as the perfect place to play board games and enjoy other leisurely activities.

A functional and inviting outdoor dining area incorporates a careful balance of many of the site considerations as well as structural and design elements described in this book. For example, ensuring privacy, sufficient shade, and shelter from the elements—with features such as shade trees, overheads, screening, and fences—will add significantly to your enjoyment of the space. Defining the area with colorful plantings will also add appeal. In general, cool colors will make you feel relaxed and meditative. Warm colors create an energized, active space. Furniture is also very important. It is discussed on page 66.

Like outdoor kitchens, dining areas are most useful when located within easy access of the house. If you have a large property, however, you may decide to create such spaces in more remote locations.

Tall trees arching overhead provide a canopy over this dining area, keeping it cool and comfortable on even the hottest summer days. This location also offers diners a full view of the swimming pool.

Plump pillows and wicker furniture add character and comfort to this sheltered and intimate dining spot. Table flowers and container plants add color and help tie the space into the larger patio area.

PLANNING YOUR DINING SPACE

Whatever your choice of furniture, you'll need to figure out how best to use your available space to make the dining area as easy to use as possible. Outdoor furniture generally takes up more space than indoor furniture and container plants take up their share of room, but most important are traffic patterns. You'll need to leave enough space for people to maneuver around the table and other furniture for serving and removing food. The illustration at right shows one example of how to calculate clearances around furniture.

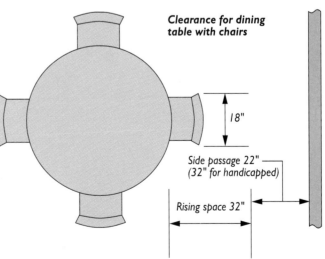

Clearance for dining table with chairs

18"

Side passage 22"
(32" for handicapped)

Rising space 32"

Picnic Table and Benches

A picnic table is a classic patio addition. The design shown below, complete with matching benches, is practical, durable, and simple to make. And by following the instructions on these two pages, there's no reason why you can't build one in time for your next cookout.

GETTING STARTED

The table and benches should be made of a rot-resistant wood such as redwood or cedar. Begin by cutting pieces A through H according to the cutting list on the page opposite. Then, lay the top pieces (A) best-side down on a clean, flat surface, in groups of two for the benches and five for the table. Space them side by side ⅛ inch apart (2½-inch box nails work well as spacers), keeping all ends flush.

JOINING THE TOPS

Set the table cleats (B) across the tabletop pieces and the bench

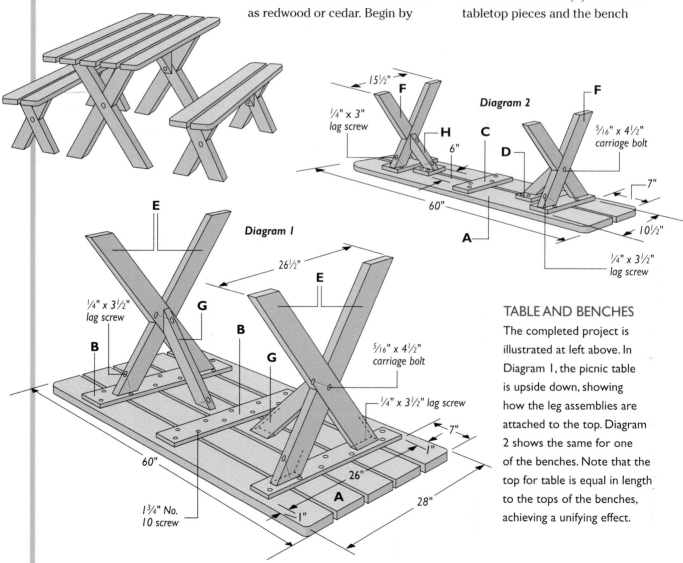

Diagram 1

Diagram 2

15½"

¼" x 3" lag screw

F

H   C

6"

D

60"

A

5⁄16" x 4½" carriage bolt

7"

10½"

¼" x 3½" lag screw

E

26½"

E

¼" x 3½" lag screw

G

B

B

G

5⁄16" x 4½" carriage bolt

¼" x 3½" lag screw

60"

7"

1"

26"

A

1¾" No. 10 screw

1"

28"

TABLE AND BENCHES

The completed project is illustrated at left above. In Diagram 1, the picnic table is upside down, showing how the leg assemblies are attached to the top. Diagram 2 shows the same for one of the benches. Note that the top for table is equal in length to the tops of the benches, achieving a unifying effect.

cleats (C) and (D) across the bench-top pieces, positioning them as shown in Diagrams 1 and 2. Drill countersunk holes for 1¾-inch No. 10 screws through the cleats and into the tops. Remove the B, C, and D pieces, remembering where they go, then spread glue on the undersides and screw them in place.

PREPARING THE LEGS

You will need to cut grooves for the interlocking joints in the table and bench legs at the points where they cross. To locate these, first drill ⁵⁄₁₆-inch holes through the legs as indicated in the detail below. Join pairs of legs by pushing carriage bolts through them. Spread them in an X shape until the distance between the bottom of them measures 26½ inches for the table legs and 15½ inches for the bench legs. Mark along their edges where they intersect.

JOINING THE LEGS

Remove the carriage bolts and cut the grooves for the interlocking joints by making a series of parallel cuts ¾ inch deep between the marks; then, chisel out the waste wood. Next, counterbore and drill pilot holes for the lag screws, then attach the table legs (E) to their braces (G) and the bench legs (F) to their braces (H).

INSTALLING THE TOPS

With the tabletop upside down, set the leg assemblies upside down on the cleats (B) and fasten the leg assemblies to the tabletop with 3½-inch lag screws and washers. Follow the same procedure for the bench tops, using 3-inch lag screws to fasten the braces (H) to the cleats (D). Turn the table and benches upright on a flat surface. If the legs tend to rock, trim them slightly. Sand all corners, edges, and surfaces, then apply two or three coats of polyurethane or penetrating-oil sealer.

Cutting details for legs and braces
The drawings above show the cutting details for the table legs (E), bench legs (F), table leg braces (G), and bench leg braces (H), and will help you cut the proper angles at the ends of each piece as well as position the lag screws and carriage bolts.

CUTTING AND MATERIALS LIST

A	Tabletop and bench tops	Nine 2x6s @ 60"
B	Table cleats	Three 1x4s @ 26"
C	Bench cleats	Six 1x4s @ 10½"
D	Bench cleats	Four 1x4s @ 6"
E	Table legs	Four 2x4s @ 36"
F	Bench legs	Eight 2x4s @ 19"
G	Table leg braces	Two 2x4s @ 20"
H	Bench leg braces	Four 2x3s @ 10½"
Carriage bolts		Six ⁵⁄₁₆" x 4½"
Lag screws		Fourteen ¼" x 3½" Four ¼" x 3"
Flathead screws		Seventy 1¾" No. 10
Nuts and washers		
Waterproof glue		
Finish or sealer		

Relaxation Areas

As you design your patio or garden environment, try to set aside one or two pleasant, secluded spots where you can stretch out and enjoy the weather, or sit and talk privately away from the house. These spaces can also function as attractive, visual focal points in a garden. Like any outdoor living space, features like screens, hedges, and other plantings can help define these spaces. A strategically placed garden bench set between container plants and against garden vines, for example, can provide a good vantage point for enjoying garden flowers or a pleasant view while serving as a striking design feature. A sturdy seat built around the base of a tree can transform an otherwise underused part of the garden into a pleasantly shaded getaway. Be sure to allow space for the expansion of the tree trunk as the tree grows. Similarly, if

A rustic bench and chairs blend effortlessly into a green forest background in this peaceful sitting area. Colorful plantings line the path back to civilization.

What better place for afternoon reading or relaxing than a comfortable hammock hung between two trees in a favorite corner of the backyard.

you decide to include a water feature on your property *(page 86)*, incorporate a sitting area nearby to enjoy this addition to its fullest.

Out-of-the-way garden spots linked to the house and other parts of the property by garden paths add a sense of mystery and surprise. As well, by providing a destination, they can allow you to show off any number of attractive features along the way.

Cushions make garden seats more comfortable and absorb heat that would otherwise make metal or plastic furniture uncomfortable.

Choose colors that pick up on color schemes in the garden. Some garden supply stores sell cushions designed for outdoor use.

Along with chaise longues and armchairs—like the one shown with plans on page 68—hammocks are another great lounging option.

HAMMOCKS

What could be more relaxing on a hot day than lying in a tree-shaded hammock as cool breezes rock you gently back and forth?

Today's hammocks have evolved beyond the familiar versions that were made of cotton rope or string and suspended between two trees. Today a wide range of styles, colors, and materials are available.

For families, hammocks come in sizes large enough to rock you and the children to a peaceful sleep. And if your yard doesn't have two trees that are sufficiently strong or at the correct distance from each other, some models can be mounted on a commercial frame.

The pictures below display a few of the hammocks you can choose from to fit your needs and garden decor perfectly. Check synthetic materials carefully before buying. Some are soft and more durable than cotton, but others may be harder on the skin.

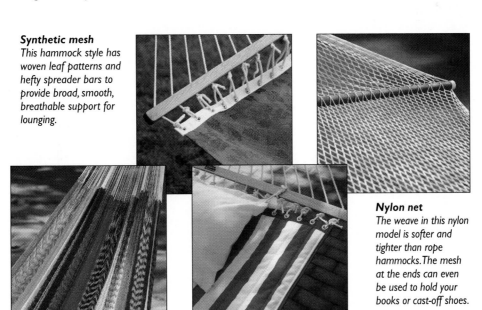

Synthetic mesh
This hammock style has woven leaf patterns and hefty spreader bars to provide broad, smooth, breathable support for lounging.

Nylon net
The weave in this nylon model is softer and tighter than rope hammocks. The mesh at the ends can even be used to hold your books or cast-off shoes.

Multicolored Mayan
This exotic style weaves almost two miles of nylon string into a sturdy, vibrant, graceful form.

Quilted and reversible
This style has batting sandwiched between striped and solid-color sides for added comfort.

Furniture Selection

Outdoor furniture is available in a huge variety of styles. As much as possible, base your color and design selections on your surroundings and garden style. For example, classic wrought-iron furniture is at home in a formal or period setting, while wooden furniture generally completes a more informal look.

Colors should either blend or contrast effectively with surrounding plantings and the color of nearby structural elements. It's a good idea to select furniture colors that echo the colors of siding or trim. Also consider that outdoor furniture may be visible from inside. In that case, consider picking colors that match those in curtain patterns.

But if it is going to see much use, your outdoor furniture should not only be stylish, but comfortable as well. Keep this in mind when shopping and be sure to try out items before buying. If you purchase a table and chairs separately, make sure that they are compatible in height, style, and color so they create an attractive set.

Brightly painted to contrast with the black garden bench, a pair of Adirondack chairs add color and classic charm to this shaded sitting area.

With a growing
selection of finish
options, aluminum
patio furniture
has become more
versatile than ever
in recent years. It
is strong, rustproof,
and stands up well
to harsh weather.

Wrought-iron furniture, with its
attention to detail, is at once elegant
and hardy enough to stand up to the
elements. Cushions can be added to
chairs for extra comfort.

Lawn Chair

If you're looking for comfort as well as styling in a piece of outdoor furniture, this classic Adirondack chair has both. With a tilted backrest and a reclining seat, it offers an inviting and relaxing place to sit, while its wide armrests provide enough surface for a few magazines or a refreshing drink.

CUT OUT THE PATTERNS

Use the grid patterns on the page opposite as a guide to cut out arm pieces (A and B) and seat legs (D)

from 1x6s. The cutting list, also shown opposite, gives the dimensions of the arms and legs as well as the other pieces of the chair. For the tapering outside back slats (G), rip and sand a 32-inch 1x3 into two identical pieces, with ends measuring ½ and 1⅞ inches wide.

START AT THE FRONT

Cut a ¾-inch-deep by 3½-inch-long dado in each front leg (E), starting 10½ inches up from the bottom. Attach the arm supports (B) so they're flush with the top and front edges of the legs, then attach

FINISHING UP

Once the chair has been assembled, it can be painted, stained, or left to its natural wood color. If you choose not to paint it, protect the wood against the elements with a nontoxic water-repellent preservative.
Design: William Crosby.

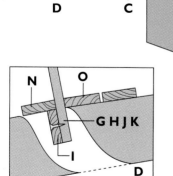

The chair is held together with waterproof glue and galvanized screws. Predrill and countersink all screw holes before assembling the chair. Here the maneuverability of a cordless drill makes the job easier.

support blocks (C) flush with the tops of the legs behind the arm supports. Attach the front stretcher (F) between the front legs; the stretcher should sit flush in the dado. Secure the seat legs (D) to the front legs so they butt against the back of stretcher F and are flush with the top edge.

SEAT AND BACK

Mount the center back slat (H) on the wide side of the 1-by-3 bottom cross brace (I), making sure the bottoms are flush. Attach two inside full slats (J) ⅝ inch from each side of H, then attach the outside full slats (K) ⅜ inch from the J pieces. Screw the ½-inch end of each of the G slats to the brace, spacing them ¼ inch from the adjacent slats. Center and screw in the upper cross brace (L) so its bottom is 27½ inches up from the bottom of the back slats.

Rip a 30° bevel along the top edge of the middle cross brace (M), then mount M 15½ inches up from the bottom of the back slats. Use a string extending to 14 inches below the top of the H slat to trace an arc in the chair back, then cut out the arc.

ATTACHING THE UNITS

Attach the 1x3 back brace (N) on the seat legs. Tuck the seat back's brace (I) under N, then screw the legs to the brace. Position the arms so they overhang the front of the supports (B) by 3 inches and the inner edges of the front legs by ¼ inch, then screw the support blocks (C) to the arms. Use single screws to attach the arms to the ends of the brace (M), making sure they're even with one another. Screw the seat legs (D) into the brace (I), then attach the N brace

to the I brace with four screws. Finally, attach the six 1x3 slats (O) ½ inch apart so the front edge of the first one is flush with the front of the stretcher.

CUTTING AND MATERIALS LIST		
A	Arm	Two 1x6s @ 28½"
B	Arm support	Two 1x6s @ 10½"
C	Support block	Two 1x3s @ 3½"
D	Seat leg	Two 1x6s @ 31½"
E	Front leg	Two 1x4s @ 21"
F	Front stretcher	One 1x4 @ 23"
G	Tapering black slat	Two 1x3s @ 32"
H	Center back slat	One 1x6 @ 35"
I	Bottom cross brace	One 1x3 @ 20"
J	Inside full slat	Two 1x3s @ 35"
K	Outside full slat	Two 1x3s @ 34"
L	Upper cross brace	One 1x2 @ 21"
M	Middle cross brace	One 1x2 @ 24"
N	Back and leg brace	One 1x3 @ 21½"
O	Seat slats	Six 1x3s @ 21½"
Galvanized flathead wood screws		1¼" No. 8 (1 box)
Waterproof glue		
Finishing materials		

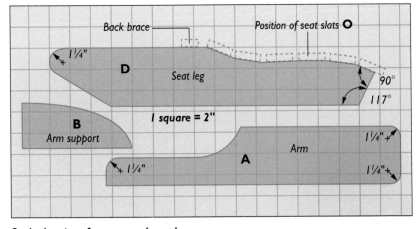

Scale drawings for arms and seat legs
In the scale drawing above, 1 square equals 2 inches. Simply enlarge the grid to produce the right-size patterns for cutting out the arms and seat legs.

Lighting the Outdoors

Garden and patio lighting should balance functional needs—such as lighting paths, steps, and doorways for safety—with the aesthetic considerations of creating atmosphere and attractive visual effects.

LIGHTING FOR SAFETY AND DECORATION

The key to satisfying both functional and decorative lighting needs is subtlety. Functional and decorative lighting should merge with the surroundings, creating small areas of light to highlight selected features.

Walks and steps: Walkways should be softly lit to avoid detracting focus from nearby decorative lighting. Low fixtures that spread soft pools of light are effective. By incorporating them into plantings along the edge of the path, you can show off elements of your garden and camouflage the fixtures during the day. Steps can be lit by these fixtures as well, or by fixtures built into the risers of the steps themselves or into a retaining wall on either side of the steps.

Dining areas and living spaces: Dim lighting is usually appropriate for quiet conversation or outdoor dining. Soft, indirect lighting provides enough visibility to see without robbing the evening of its

OUTDOOR LIGHTING TECHNIQUES

Shown here are several standard outdoor lighting techniques. You can combine techniques for interesting results. For example, a moonlight effect can be achieved by placing both uplights and downlights in a large tree. Remember that in cooking areas you'll need stronger lights than you will for lounging.

Downlighting
Use this technique to gently light up porches, patios, and walkways. It's also good for accenting trees, flowers, and shrubs, while providing enough light at night to maneuver.

Spread lighting
Light up your shrubbery with spread lights placed in the planting beds themselves.

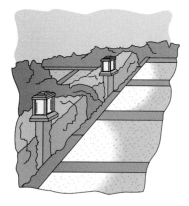

Path lighting
Low fixtures that spread soft pools of light can define a walkway and highlight elements of the garden. For some, this "runway" effect can seem too contrived. Alternatively you can light paths indirectly using the other techniques shown.

Diffused lighting
A low level of lighting is often enough for low-traffic areas. Light railings and fences indirectly from underneath or behind to outline the edges of the structures.

"Moonlighting"
Used to approximate the normal effect of moonlight, uplights and downlights placed within the branches of a tree will provide enough light to distinguish the tree from the rest of the landscape, but not enough to call harsh attention to itself.

With effective lighting, this gazebo and tree unite to produce a magical summer-evening atmosphere. The gazebo is lit from within by light fixtures tucked away in the roof, while the tree is illuminated using the "moonlighting" technique described opposite.

mood. Cooking and other activity areas require brighter lighting.

Foliage: Uplighting, downlighting, and spread lighting (shown opposite) are common techniques for illuminating foliage. Using separate switches and dimmers allows a greater variation of lighting effects.

For a dappled "moonlight" effect, place both uplights and downlights in a large tree to highlight some of the foliage and create shadows on the ground. To silhouette a tree or shrub, aim a spotlight or wall washer at a fence or a wall from close behind the plant. Decorative mini-lights can be used to outline trees and other features while lending sparkle to the garden.

AVOIDING GLARE

Avoiding glare, either through light placement or fixture selection, is important for both functional and decorative lighting. Glare is responsible for the discomfort we feel when looking at a light that is too bright or that is aimed straight at our eyes.

Placing and directing fixtures: The best way to avoid glare is to place fixtures out of sight lines, either very low or very high: along a walk or up in a tree, for example. Then, direct the fixtures so that only the effect of the light is noticed. Avoid creating bright spots of light.

Using more fixtures: It's both less glaring and more inviting to use a few strategically placed lower-wattage lights outside a door than using one high-wattage light.

Using shielded fixtures: In a shielded fixture, the bulb area is completely hidden by a shroud that directs the light away from viewers' eyes. The eye instead sees the warm glow of a lighted

Slightly raised light fixtures highlight plantings, provide a sense of depth, and improve safety and security in this space.

The light produced by nearby entry spotlights and step lights is "recycled" through architectural panels that do triple duty as privacy screens, wind breaks, and a glare-free light source.

object rather than a concentrated hot spot of light.

OUTDOOR LIGHTING SYSTEMS

Low-voltage lighting systems *(below)* are frequently used out-doors. Compared to standard 120-volt systems, they are safer to use, require less energy to run, and can be installed by nonprofessionals.

Standard 120-volt lighting systems should be installed by an electrician, but have the advantage of accommodating lights with a wider beam spread as well as long-lasting, high-intensity-discharge (HID) bulbs. In addition, power tools can be plugged into 120-volt outlets.

Adding a Low-Voltage Lighting System

To install a low-voltage system for outdoor use, you'll need a transformer, usually housed in a waterproof box, to step the household current of 120 volts down to 12 volts. Mount the transformer near the watertight switch or receptacle and run a cable a few inches below the ground from the low-voltage side of the transformer to the desired locations for your lights. Some fixtures simply clip onto the wire, while others must be wired into the system. Some low-voltage lights come in a kit with a transformer. Be sure to use the right size of wire given in the instructions. If you don't already have an outlet to plug the transformer into, have an electrician install a GFCI-protected outlet *(below)*.

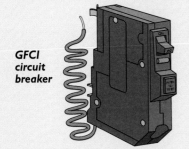

GFCI circuit breaker

GFCI protection
According to present electrical codes, any new outside receptacle must be protected by a ground-fault circuit interrupter (GFCI or GFI). Whenever the amounts of incoming and outgoing current are not equal—indicating current leakage (a "ground fault")—the GFCI opens the circuit instantly, cutting off the power.

GFCI receptacle

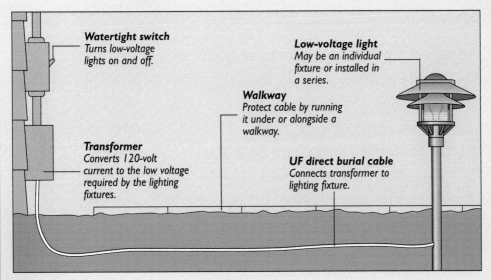

Watertight switch
Turns low-voltage lights on and off.

Transformer
Converts 120-volt current to the low voltage required by the lighting fixtures.

Walkway
Protect cable by running it under or alongside a walkway.

Low-voltage light
May be an individual fixture or installed in a series.

UF direct burial cable
Connects transformer to lighting fixture.

A typical 12-volt installation
Since a 12-volt system uses a greatly reduced voltage, special conduit and boxes of other outdoor wiring are not required. Most transformers are rated for home use from 100 to 300 watts. The higher the rating, the more lengths of 100-foot cable—and the more light fixtures—that can be connected to the transformer. Most transformers are encased in watertight boxes; to be safe, plan to install yours at least a foot off the ground in a sheltered, convenient location.

Adding
COLOR AND
SPARKLE

Trees and plants, including shrubs, perennials, and annuals, bring color and life to outdoor living spaces and serve a range of practical and design functions. Depending on how they're used, plants can create a wide range of effects, drawing the eye away from unpleasant views or making a space seem larger or smaller. The following chapter offers tips for taming an overgrown garden and valuable advice on incorporating all types of new plantings successfully. Finally, this chapter contains design and installation guidelines for simple garden water features, the perfect finishing touch in any well-planned garden environment.

Garden Remodeling

As you develop your plans to improve or create new outdoor garden and patio living spaces, you may find that your present garden requires considerable remodeling before it can begin to form the backdrop for your intended design. The following pages contain some simple ideas you can put to use to bring dramatic new life to your garden living space.

Over the years, a backyard can become a jungle as overgrown shrubs choke once open spaces and tall trees block out the sun.

The first step in remodeling such a garden is to move in with a saw and pruning shears. Open up shapeless shrubs by removing branches, not simply shearing the plant's outer edges. Removing about every third branch will reduce the size of the plant but maintain its natural shape. Prune tangled vines and remove plants too big for their space. In certain cases—for example, if you're planning to incorporate a formal garden design—you may have to clear the area of all existing vegetation.

In addition to your ultimate design plans, having young children may determine whether or not a

GARDEN STYLES

The illustrations below show four distinct approaches to garden design. Although you don't have to decide in advance what every plant will be and where it will go, having a general design or theme will help you select plants and set them out in harmonious arrangements.

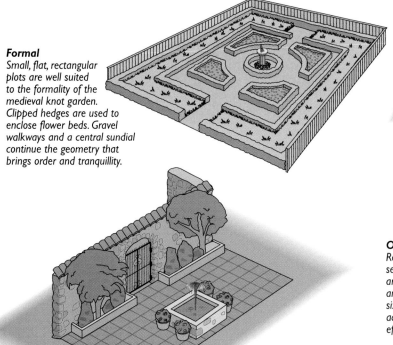

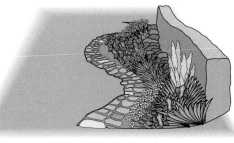

Formal
Small, flat, rectangular plots are well suited to the formality of the medieval knot garden. Clipped hedges are used to enclose flower beds. Gravel walkways and a central sundial continue the geometry that brings order and tranquillity.

Cottage
For centuries the English have excelled at packing an astonishing variety of annuals and perennials into a small space with great effect. Various plants can be chosen based on harmonizing colors and then set off against the deep green of a serpentine hedge.

Oriental
Restraint and simplicity result in the desired serenity of this style of garden. A naturalistic arrangement of rocks and gravel and a few plants of varying size and texture achieve the effect.

Spanish
The courtyard of a Spanish-style house, with its central fountain, adobe walls, and wrought-iron grillwork, becomes a cool, formal oasis with a few careful plantings of shrubs and dwarf trees.

plant should stay. Poisonous or thorny plants can be a hazard for youngsters and pets. As well, plants that bear fruits can cause stained walks, walls, and interior carpets.

Next, thin out the canopy overhead to allow sunlight to penetrate to the undergrowth and help it develop. For your safety and the health of your trees, consider hiring an arborist to do any high pruning. On selected trees, prune bottom branches to create high shade for outdoor sitting areas, if appropriate to your final plan. Once you've created this basic living framework, you can use the remaining sections of this chapter to bring new life to your outdoor spaces by adding plants, water features, and other decorative elements.

BEFORE/AFTER VIEWS

The five sets of illustrations below and opposite are intended to give you an understanding of how you can revitalize the look of an old garden with plants and other decorative features.

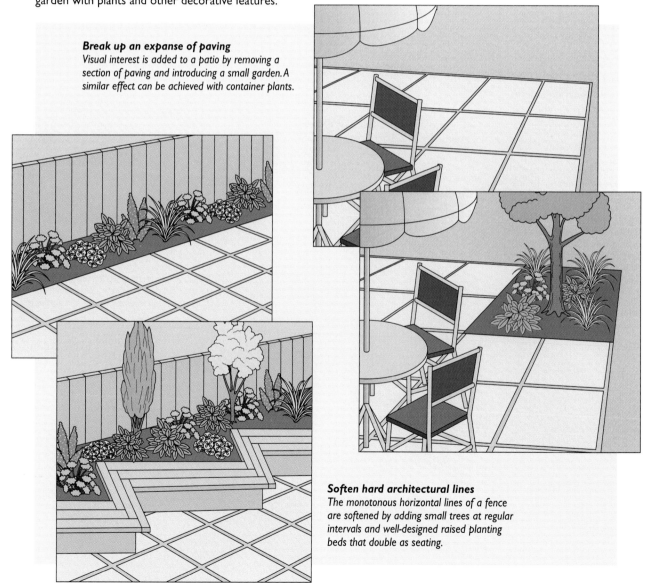

Break up an expanse of paving
Visual interest is added to a patio by removing a section of paving and introducing a small garden. A similar effect can be achieved with container plants.

Soften hard architectural lines
The monotonous horizontal lines of a fence are softened by adding small trees at regular intervals and well-designed raised planting beds that double as seating.

Add reflection or silhouette

Textures and forms of certain plants are magnified when they are reflected in a garden pool or outlined in silhouette against a dark wall. Plants with distinctive textures and forms include Japanese maple, bamboo, and tropical fatsia.

Sculpt with plantings

Properly pruned, a plant can become a living sculpture. Here three straight, slender trees make a strong visual statement along a curved walkway. Sculptural possibilities include plants with interesting branch structure, bonsai, a wind-carved tree, or shrubs pruned to create interesting shapes (excellent topiary choices include boxwood, privet, and yew).

Frame an area

A semicircle of hedge around this small patio gives a sense of intimacy without complete confinement. This kind of partial screening delineates space without blocking out desired views.

Trees, Shrubs, and Hedges

If you try to imagine your landscape without trees, shrubs, or hedges, you'll quickly begin to grasp the importance of these items in the look and day-to-day enjoyment of your property.

The simplest way to differentiate shrubs from trees is that you walk around one and under the other. More technical differences exist, but applying them can be complicated since some plants can be classified as either tree or shrub, depending on how they are pruned.

Among their many decorative and practical functions, trees, shrubs, and hedges can define patio and garden areas, provide privacy, shelter, and shade, create focal points, block out undesirable elements, and frame attractive views.

SELECTING TREES AND SHRUBS

Selecting trees and shrubs for your garden depends largely on the function you want them to perform and on local climate conditions. (For a complete list of garden trees and shrubs, along with their general characteristics and climate zones, see Sunset's *Trees and Shrubs*.)

• If you're looking for a shade tree, you can eliminate a great many species and concentrate on those with a sizeable canopy.

• To screen the sight line from your neighbor's second story, choose tall, dense shrubs or short trees with foliage at the right height.

• If you want a tree for a screen or a windbreak, study the various types of indigenous evergreens whose foliage will protect you for the entire year or the time of year when you need protection.

• Appropriate trees for patios and small gardens grow slowly and to a limited size, requiring little corrective pruning. Good patio trees do not create a large amount of litter from leaves, fruits, or blossoms, and have root systems that won't buckle paving or prevent other plants from growing beneath them.

• To create a focal point, look for trees and shrubs that are the right

A tall hedge provides a high degree of privacy, without being as imposing as a fence of the same height. The shrubs also visually soften and cool the area.

A carefully selected variety of trees and shrubs encircles a garden pond with appealing colors, shapes, and textures. The taller trees also help block out unwanted views.

size for the site and that offer a display of flowers, fruits, or unusually attractive foliage. Pruning shrubs into eye-catching shapes is another way to create a focal point, but requires frequent pruning to keep the plants shapely.

• When choosing shrubs for a hedge, decide whether you want to let the hedge grow high and thick or trim it carefully for a more formal look (this works best for shrubs with dense foliage that begins at ground level).

Growth rate and size: How quickly or slowly a tree or shrub reaches a significant size is always a vital factor whenever a landscape problem demands a quick solution. The need for shade or privacy may push you toward selecting a fast-growing plant, but when the need is purely for beauty you can afford to wait longer for fulfillment. If budget and access permit, very large plants can be installed from the start.

PLANTING TREES AND SHRUBS

Successful tree and shrub planting depends on choosing the best time of year to do the work (which will vary according to where you live and the plant you choose) and on using the correct planting technique.

Climate: In colder climates, best first-year growth, with the least amount of stress on the new tree or shrub, calls for planting in advance of the spring growing season while the soil is cool—although planting is possible into the late fall.

In milder climates where the ground freezes seldom or not at all, autumn through winter is the preferred planting period.

Soil: The practice of amending soil when planting trees has virtually disappeared. Research shows that trees in bare-root or balled-and-burlapped form grow best when the planting hole is backfilled with excavated native soil. For shrubs, it is a good idea to amend the soil by adding organic matter. Check with your county extension service for the best type to use. For trees and shrubs, make sure the hole is at least twice as wide as the roots and cover the planting area with 2 to 3 inches of mulch when finished. Compost, shredded hardwood, and bark mulch are good options.

Planting balled-and-burlapped plants

1 Digging the hole
Dig a hole for the root ball slightly shallower and at least two times wider than the root ball or root system of the plant it will receive *(right)*. The sides of the hole should taper inward as shown.

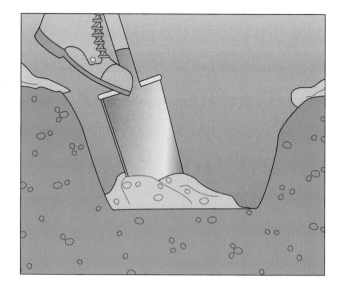

2 Positioning the plant
Set the plant in its hole, placing the root ball on the firm plateau at the center *(left)*. The top of the root ball should extend about 2 inches above the surrounding soil.

3 Filling the hole
Untie the burlap and spread it out to uncover about half of the root ball. Backfill half the hole, then water the plant to eliminate air pockets. (If planting a shrub, amend the soil with organic matter.) If the plant is located in a windy area, you may need to stake it. If so, drive a stake into the soil alongside the root ball *(right)*. (The burlap will eventually decay.)

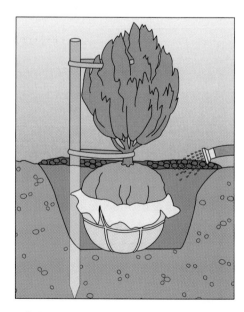

4 Securing and watering the plant
Refill the hole to the top with backfill. Then, if the plant is staked, loosely tie it to the stake. Add a 2- to 3-inch layer of mulch. Finally, water the plant thoroughly *(above)*.

Splashes of Color

Flowers and colorful plants bring patio and garden living spaces to life and can produce an endless variety of design effects.

Color can be used to increase or decrease a feeling of space, create a mood, or show off your personality. Flowers can also help tie structural and design elements into a unified whole. For example, if you have added a wall, fence, or hedge to set apart or enclose a living space, these features can act as a perfect backdrop to show off a bank of colorful blooms. Similarly, you can soften the look of a patio over-head by hanging flowering container plants from posts or rafters.

COLOR CONSIDERATIONS

The same general rules apply for selecting garden colors as for combining decorative colors inside the house. Plantings should emphasize a continuous segment of the color wheel *(page 82)*: red, red-violet, and violet, for example. The smaller the area, the narrower this segment should be. Use complementary colors—colors that appear opposite each other on the color wheel—for accents. You can also create strik-ing contrasts with the occasional use of light and dark colors togeth-er—for example, light yellow marigolds with dark blue lobelia. If you think two colors may clash when located side by side, separate them with white.

Vibrant oranges, yellows, and reds draw the eye and are effective for creating distant focal points. This can be useful to divert attention away from a less pleasant view, but otherwise can overshadow attractive features in the foreground.

The cool colors of the green-blue-violet range, on the other hand, can

In a variation on the cottage-garden design, a sweeping bank of flowers rises in a succession of colorful levels. The flowers closest to the ground highlight the curve of the lawn while the taller plantings create a sense of privacy and enclosure.

COLOR WHEEL

Use the color wheel shown at right as a guide when planting. As a rule, work with adjacent colors on the color wheel. Save complementary colors—those opposite each other—for accents.

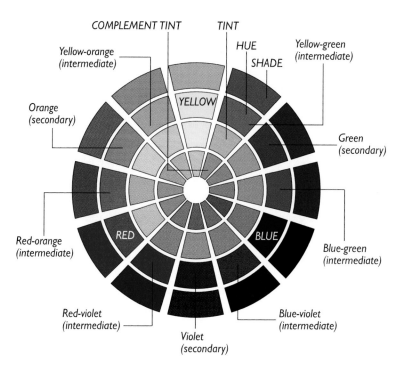

COMPLEMENT TINT
TINT
HUE
SHADE
Yellow-orange (intermediate)
Yellow-green (intermediate)
Orange (secondary)
YELLOW
Green (secondary)
Red-orange (intermediate)
RED
BLUE
Blue-green (intermediate)
Red-violet (intermediate)
Violet (secondary)
Blue-violet (intermediate)

make a shallow space appear deeper; these work best when grouped.

To lessen the sense of enclosure in a smaller garden area, plant light colors at the borders. In general, the eye stops at dark colors (and as such they can create or add to a sense of confinement), while the opposite is true of light colors. To brighten large areas, strategic use of warm reds, oranges, and yellows can be effective.

In addition to flowers, foliage provides a wide spectrum of colors as well as many different shades of green that can also be combined to great effect.

Always use restraint when planting a garden. An attractive landscape should be restful to the eye. A range of muted colors, with occasional accents, is far more attractive and calming than a riot of contrasting bright colors.

FLOWER SELECTION

To keep your garden colorful throughout the growing season and over successive years, choose flowers that have different bloom times and life cycles, and envision how they will change the look of your garden over time. Annuals are fast-growing plants that thrive for one season and then die. Biennials devel-

op foliage the first year then bloom and die the second. Perennials flower for more than two summers. Bulbs sprout roots, leaves, and flowers each spring, summer, or fall, depending on the variety. One good plan is to locate spring bloomers in one area, summer bloomers in another, and fall bloomers in yet another. This shifts focus from one area to another with each season.

In addition to flowers, carefully select foliage plants that will provide a contrasting backdrop for colorful blooms. The shapes and textures of plants and flowers should also be a consideration. In general, fine-textured plants create a restful, pastoral feeling while coarse textures add energy and life.

Fragrance is an important but often overlooked factor in selecting plant and flower combinations. Fragrant plants require warm, sheltered spots to fully reveal their scent. With this in mind, consider

creating a fragrance zone in a sheltered place near a sitting area where you can best enjoy the scents.

Other good places for fragrant plants are along garden paths and near doors or windows (allowing scents to waft into the house).

CONTAINERS AND RAISED BEDS

Plants in containers and hanging pots are great decorative touches for living spaces. Annuals or perennials (and even shrubs and vegetables) can be moved about like pieces in a puzzle until the desired effect is achieved (trays with casters make the moving easier). And you can give your space a new look several times a year to show off the best of the growing season.

Bringing flowers closer to eye level, raised beds are great for defining outdoor living spaces by providing pronounced borders. They are often used to break up sloping lawns.

Raised plant beds—some built with bricks, others of landscape timbers—create precise divisions between patio living spaces and garden areas. A series of raised beds like the ones on the right side of the path are an attractive way to create a terraced garden on a sloped property.

Flowering plants, trees, and shrubs in planters bring color and variety to an outdoor sitting area. Planters can be moved about over the growing season to show off various plants at their best.

Vines

In landscaping, vines are often the best choice for places where no other plant will grow. A long, blank, sunbaked wall with a walk beside it can be softened by covering it with vines. Vines can be cultivated to grow on a fence, giving some of the effect of a hedge while requiring less space and maintenance. They can also be grown on overheads to provide shade.

When selecting from the wide variety of vines available, base your choices on site considerations, rate of growth, fragrance, and the surface to be covered. Many vines have aerial roots that can damage wood, painted surfaces, and even some brick walls. (For a list of vines and their characteristics, see Sunset's *Landscaping Illustrated*.)

Most vines have certain characteristics that make climbing easy— twining stems, tendrils, or rootlets along the stems. Others have no way of holding on. But this does not necessarily mean they are harder to manage since these species can be tied into place.

The tie to use depends on the vine and the kind of structure supporting it. For a lightweight vine, use soft twine, raffia, wide rubber bands, or plastic or reinforced paper ties. These ties can also be used as an adjunct to a vine's own holding mechanism to help give the plant a head start. By the time the ties weather and give way, the twining stems or tendrils will be holding the vine in place.

For heavy-stemmed vines, particularly those that have no device for holding on, use a heavier tying material such as pliable insulated wire, heavy-rubber tree ties, sections of clothesline (woven cotton or plastic-covered), or strips of canvas. Hardware stores and home building centers also offer many heavy-duty materials to choose from, including eye screws, eye lags, and other hardware that is generally intended for different purposes.

A lush cover of vines brings an added dimension of greenery to a small enclosed patio. By absorbing the sun's rays, vines also keep the patio and interior of the house cooler.

Turf Grasses and Groundcovers

Lawns of grass and other groundcovers are a popular way to bring color to large open spaces, at the same time providing a softer look and feel than paving. A lawn acts as a backdrop for contrasting garden elements or links related parts of a design by providing a uniform base. Some regard a lawn as a stage that allows the rest of the landscape to perform.

GRASSES

Any one of dozens of grass species can be planted to create a lawn. These range from delicate, fine-leafed varieties that produce a smooth, bowling-green surface to rugged, broad-leafed species that can stand up to heavy traffic. Fine-textured lawns are generally considered formal; coarse-textured, more informal. If you live in an area where adequate water is a problem, consider grasses that require less water and/or limit grass areas.

You can start a new lawn by laying strips of sod or planting seeds. Sod is much more expensive, but it is quicker to install and establishes itself much sooner. Another advantage to sod is its usefulness under trees. Because sod roots are already established, sod is more likely to prosper where seeds would be thwarted by tree roots.

Like other plants, grasses need care (cutting, fertilizing, weeding, watering, and raking) to remain healthy. Avoid cutting grass too short or it will dry out. Also, every other time you cut the grass, change the direction in which you mow. Following the same pattern with every mowing may cause discolored lines on the lawn.

GROUNDCOVERS

Groundcovers offer a uniform carpet of green (and other colors) while requiring far less maintenance than regular lawns (occasional pruning is virtually all that's needed). They will also grow in places where grasses won't.

Some types of groundcovers (ivy, pachysandra, and epimedium, for example) are tough enough to grow in the shade and withstand limited foot traffic. On areas that will not be walked on, other groundcovers offer possibilities—such as combinations of delicate wild grasses and wildflowers. Herbs like chamomile and thyme are other pleasantly fragrant alternatives.

A low-maintenance alternative to grass, this selection of groundcovers of varied colors and textures adds visual interest to sections of a lawn that would be difficult to mow.

Garden Water Features

Water features bring sparkle to the outdoors and open up a world of new planting possibilities for the avid gardener. A water feature can be as simple as a birdbath or as elaborate as an artificial waterfall. Some of the most popular garden water features are discussed below.

Garden pools: Even if you don't have the time, money, or space to build an elaborate pool, you may still be able to create a smaller, ornamental version (see the page opposite).

For a small garden pond, a depth of about 24 inches is sufficient. But for fish, a deeper pond is required because it is more difficult for predators such as raccoons and skunks to raid. A pond built primarily for fish should be placed where it will get some shade during the course of the day. This is good for the fish—their colors tend to be richer and deeper if given shade—and reduces algae. However, you may need to compromise as aquatic plants require sun.

Tub gardens: By filling a watertight wooden barrel—or other appropriate container—with water and placing it in a sunny spot, you can quickly and easily introduce the appeal of a miniature water garden to the outdoors.

A standard water lily or lotus requires a container at least 18 inches across; a 25-gallon container is a good choice for most plants. You can line containers with pond liner or hide a less attractive watertight container in a more appealing tub, trough, or barrel.

Fountains: Even the simplest fountain provides the soothing, musical effect of moving water. In addition to entertaining with sound and motion, a fountain aerates pond water, providing fresh oxygen to plants and fish, and provides benefits to people by cooling surrounding air and covering up outside noise with the relaxing sound of running water.

Fountains are available in a variety of styles, from spray fountains, which use water in opposition to gravity to create picturesque patterns, to spill fountains, typically created with a water pipe that pours water into a single container or into a series of containers on a wall so that water spills over from one to the next.

A bubbling fountain and garden pond create a focal point in this rustic, colorful garden. Wide flagstones hold down and conceal the edges of the pond liner.

A Garden Pond

One of the easiest ways for a do-it-yourselfer to build a garden pond is with a flexible pond liner.

To determine the size of the liner you need, outline the shape of the pond using a flexible hose or a chalk line. Then, draw an imaginary rectangle around it and measure the maximum length and width. To these measurements, add twice the pond's depth plus 2 feet to cover the edge of the hole.

A pond usually needs a pump to maintain water quality. The unit shown below, one of many types available, serves as both pump and fountain and is plugged into a GFCI receptacle *(page 73)*.

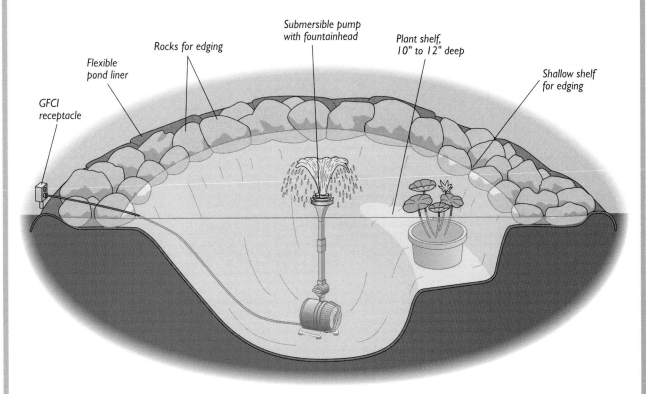

GFCI
receptacle

Flexible
pond liner

Rocks for edging

Submersible pump
with fountainhead

Plant shelf,
10" to 12" deep

Shallow shelf
for edging

Building a Garden Pond

Outline the shape of the pond, then dig around the outline. Dig a shallow shelf around the pond so that the rocks that hold down the liner edges will be partially submerged and conceal the liner. Next, dig out plant shelves (if desired); 10 to 12 inches wide is common. Continue digging, measuring depth with a marked stake. If you're planning to lay a sand bed under the liner, dig an extra 2 inches. Check the rim for level with a long, straight 2x4 and a carpenter's level, or use a line level or a water level. Remove all rough edges from the hole (rocks, branches, and so on). Add a sand bed or landscaping fabric to protect the liner and soften the bottom of the pool. Smooth the surface with a board. Spread the liner loosely over the hole (corners may need to be pleated), eliminating air pockets underneath. With the pool completed, set the fountain pump in place and begin filling the pool. When the pond is nearly full, lay flat-bottomed rocks at the edges to hold down and hide the liner and to conceal the pump's electrical cord.

Garden
WORK STRUCTURES

Elsewhere in this book, we look at garden structures such as overheads, gazebos, and other features that increase enjoyment of outdoor leisure time. This chapter provides a mix of information, ideas, and building instructions for greenhouses, garden work centers, and sheds—structures that serve the more avid gardener. Garden work centers bring a sense of organization to gardening by providing a place to store tools, potting soil, and other gardening materials. Greenhouses allow gardeners to create a controlled growing environment. For their part, sheds provide useful storage for backyard and patio equipment close to where it's needed. While such structures are primarily built for their usefulness and versatility, with good design, creative painting, and thoughtful landscaping, they can add a whole new dimension to your outdoor living areas.

Garden Work Centers

If you plan to do any serious gardening, you'll likely find a garden work center an invaluable addition to your property.

A garden work center serves as a central place for storing gardening tools and materials, and provides counter or table space for potting and other gardening work. The typical features of a garden work center include a potting counter, bins or other containers for fertilizer and potting material, a sink, racks for tools and pots, and small shelves for seeds and bottles.

The best garden work centers are planned to meet the specific needs of the home gardener, and often they must fit into a limited space. While it's possible to adapt a shed to the purpose, working inside a dark shed on a sunny day is an unappealing idea for most gardeners. A better idea is using one side of a shed's exterior to support a small work center like the ones shown on page 90.

The four work centers on the next page are designed to suit a variety of different situations. Adapt them to your needs or let them inspire you to create your own design. With the exception of the unit built into the retaining wall, they are designed to be supported by the side of a fence, shed, or garage. In most cases, work centers should be located in an unobtrusive spot where they won't detract from the larger garden design but where they are still convenient to garden areas.

The more elaborate garden work center, shown with building plans on pages 92 and 93, incorporates a large latticework screen to conceal the work area from the house and display areas.

Protected by a clear acrylic roof and equipped with a work surface, ample storage space, and hooks for hanging tools, this work center represents a paragon of practicality. Lattice panels at eye level add a decorative touch.

GARDEN WORK CENTER IDEAS

For any part of a garden work center that is close to or in contact with the ground, select redwood or cedar heartwood, or pressure-treated lumber. Make work surfaces reasonably weatherproof, sturdy, and easy to clean. To avoid creating a muddy patch of grass beneath your feet, lay a gravel floor, or consider brick, stone, or concrete—they're easier to clean.

Attached to a fence, this workbench has an overhead that shades the work area and swings down to protect plants. The shelf below holds pots, seed flats, and soil mix.

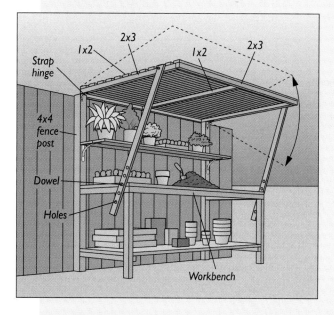

A wall-hung box with hinged front stores equipment and provides a worktable for potting and small jobs. Removable legs, held in place with dowels, can be stored in the cabinet—if there's space—or in a nearby shed or garage.

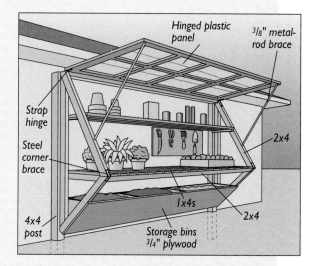

A landscape-timber bunker set down in the ground with planting beds mounded around it provides a hidden work center. Shelves of 2x12s supported on cleats provide work surfaces and storage.

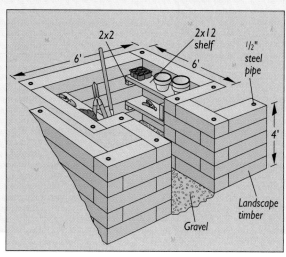

Attached to a garage wall, this work center has a hinged overhead with plastic panels, plus storage bins beneath the counter. By lowering the overhead, the work center can become a temporary cold frame.

90

Lattice panels and hanging pots help hide the clutter that is an unavoidable part of gardening. Just 2 feet deep, this garden work center has four interconnected modules. The unit also has two center bays with storage cabinets below plywood counters and a tool storage cabinet. Depending on needs and available space, the design can be modified by reducing the number of modules.

Building a Garden Work Center

This versatile garden work center is assembled from three H-shaped leg modules connected with horizontal wood spacers. At 8 feet long, both the tabletop and shelf can be cut from a single piece of exterior-grade plywood. The sheet-metal cover can be fabricated at a sheet-metal shop for about $50 and is fas-

tened to the tabletop edges with sheet-metal screws through 1-inch front and end lips.

BUILDING THE LEG MODULES

Begin the project by cutting all the pieces to length. Then, on one face of each front (A) and rear (B) leg, use a combination square to draw horizontal lines to mark the top of

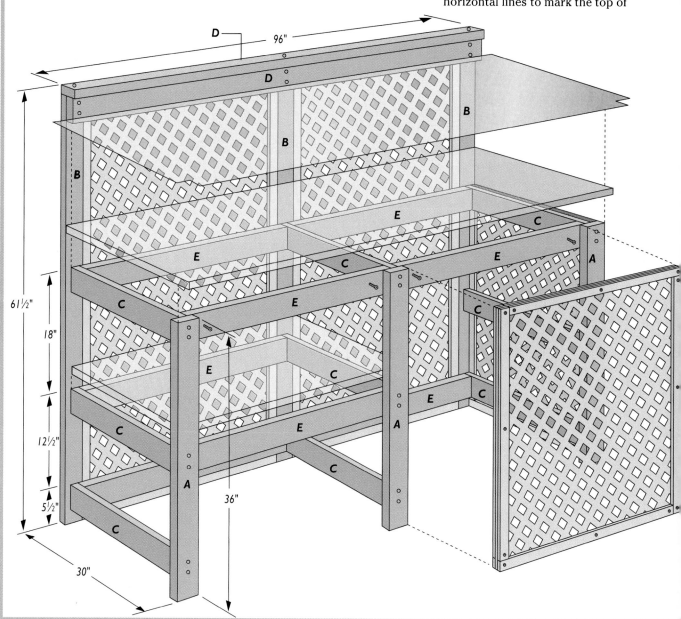

each crosspiece (C). (Their heights are indicated in the anatomy illustration on the page opposite.) Crosspieces are attached to the legs with two screws at every joint. Use an electric drill to bore $1/16$-inch pilot holes through the legs, then fasten them to the crosspieces with deck screws.

JOINING THE MODULES

Lay two leg modules on their backs, spacing their inside edges 89 inches apart. Make sure they're parallel, then join them with an 8-foot-long 2x4 cross support (D) that's flush with their tops. Use two deck screws per module. Center and add the third module. Stand the joined pieces on their legs and check the unit for square, measuring diagonally across each opening. (These measurements will match when the unit is square.) Butt six of the horizontal spacers (E) between the bottom rear, top rear, and top front

crosspieces. Screw them to the front or rear legs with two screws at every joint. (Refer to Diagram 1 for the correct location of screws at each joint.) Add the remaining two as shelf supports on the left or right side between the crosspieces. Then, screw the remaining 2x4 cross support (D) flat across the top of the frame.

PAINT FRAME/ATTACH LATTICE

Cut plastic lattice for the back, side, and front panels so they will fit snugly in their openings, then attach lattice trim. (Note: One front and one side lattice panel are removed from the anatomy illustration for clarity.) Screw the lattice panels in place with sheet-metal screws to check the fit, then remove them. Paint the wood frame with exterior paint or stain. When dry, reattach the lattice panels with screws. Hang the front lattice panels in place from screws for easy access to the storage bays.

ATTACH THE TOP AND SHELF

Set the top (F) on the top spacers to check alignment and squareness of the modules, then set it aside. Nail the shelf in place. Nail the plywood top to the frame, then slip on the metal top, fold over the front and end lips, and secure it with sheet-metal screws into the edge of the top. Solder the corners, then file them smooth. If you can't solder, cover the corners with metal clips or L brackets screwed into the top.

CUTTING AND MATERIALS LIST		
A Front legs	Three 2x4s @ 36"	
B Rear legs	Three 2x4s @ 60"	
C Crosspieces	Nine 2x4s @ 27"	
D Cross supports	Two 2x4s @ 96"	
E Horizontal spacers	Eight 2x4s @ $44^{3}/_{4}$"	
F Top	$3/_{4}$" plywood @ 29" x 96"	
G Shelf	$3/_{4}$" plywood @ 27" x $47^{3}/_{4}$"	
H Lattice side panels	Plastic lattice @ 27" x 34"	
I Lattice rear panels	Plastic lattice @ $42^{3}/_{4}$" x 58"	
J Lattice front panels	Plastic lattice @ $42^{3}/_{4}$" x 34"	
Lattice trim	Eleven pieces @ 8' (cut to size)	
Deck screws	94 @ $2^{1}/_{4}$"	
Sheet-metal screws	32 @ $2^{1}/_{4}$"	
Galvanized finishing nails	24 @ 2"	

Diagram I
In this modular design, crosspieces (C) are centered on the legs (A), leaving room for spacers (E) to be added later. The frame components are assembled with $2^{1}/_{4}$" deck screws.

Greenhouses

Most gardeners wish they could control the weather. By providing a space where the elements can be carefully monitored and adjusted to create ideal growing conditions, greenhouses, on a small scale, allow them to do just that.

CHOOSING A GREENHOUSE

At its simplest, a greenhouse is a frame with transparent material, or glazing. Framing materials range from lightweight polyvinylchloride (PVC) pipe to sturdier options such as wood, galvanized metal, and steel pipe. The most common types of glazing are plastic sheeting, fiberglass, and glass. Your choices of glazing and framing material will depend on several factors, the most important being how you plan to use the greenhouse. If your goal is simply to extend the growing season by a few weeks in the spring and fall, a unit made of PVC pipe and plastic sheeting will do the trick and fit most budgets. Units covered with plastic have the added advantage of being considered as temporary structures, meaning they are given a lower tax-assessment rate. Bear in mind, however, that PVC pipe will break down relatively quickly when exposed to ultraviolet light. If you want a more durable structure, you should choose stronger materials for both the framing and glazing. Often the type of glazing will determine the material you use for the frame as well as the type of foundation you provide for the structure. Glass glazing, for example, requires the support of heavier framing, typically galvanized metal or wood. In colder climates, glass greenhouses require a foundation that extends below the frost line—otherwise the glass may crack when the ground heaves during temperature shifts. If you use fiberglass glazing, choose the highest grade available. Lower grades tend to discolor over time.

In addition to materials, greenhouses are divided by whether they

A freestanding glass greenhouse provides a year-round facility for the avid gardener. With the greenhouse's long side walls facing east and west, the plants receive a balance of sunlight during the course of a day.

are freestanding or house-attached. Although freestanding greenhouses can be equipped for year-round use, they are extremely costly to heat and cool, and are usually not used during the hottest and coldest months of the year. They are commonly made with PVC pipe and plastic sheeting, with little or no foundation. Ventilation is provided by opening doors or rolling up the plastic. House-attached greenhouses, on the other hand, typically function more like an extra room, with a sturdy foundation, heavy-duty framing, and glass glazing. They are more permanent structures (and more expensive to build), and they can usually be used year-round. A third, extremely low-cost option is the cold frame (see sidebar below).

Regardless of the type of greenhouse you choose, unless you're experienced with construction, you should leave the building to a professional. Greenhouse kits, which come ready for assembly, are the exception. They area available in a wide range of designs from home and garden centers as well as greenhouse supply stores.

SITE SELECTION

Freestanding greenhouses are typically oriented with their short sides facing north and south, so that the long axis of the building receives morning sun on one side and afternoon sun on the other. It's also important to check that there are no trees, hills, or buildings to the south, southeast, or southwest of the structure that would throw shade—unless they are far away or low to the ground. When possible, attached greenhouses are built on the south side of a house.

Other site considerations include level grading, drainage, proximity to sources of water and electricity, and distances from the garden and tool shed.

CONTROLLING THE GREENHOUSE ENVIRONMENT

Successful plant growth depends on controlling heat, ventilation, shade, and watering.

Heat and shade: It is sometimes possible to connect an attached greenhouse to your home heating system. A heating contractor can tell you whether your system has

Cold Frames

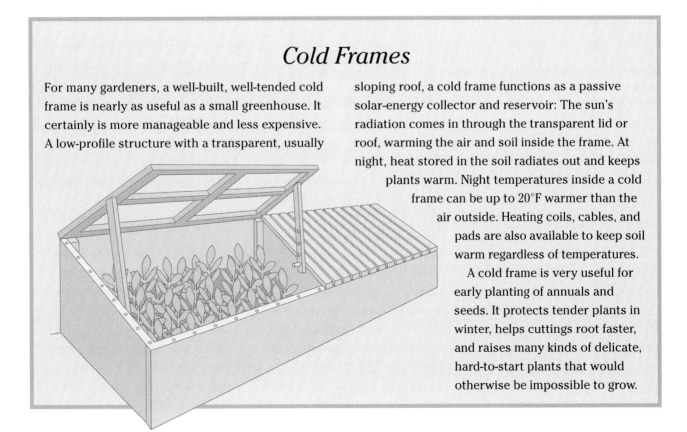

For many gardeners, a well-built, well-tended cold frame is nearly as useful as a small greenhouse. It certainly is more manageable and less expensive. A low-profile structure with a transparent, usually sloping roof, a cold frame functions as a passive solar-energy collector and reservoir: The sun's radiation comes in through the transparent lid or roof, warming the air and soil inside the frame. At night, heat stored in the soil radiates out and keeps plants warm. Night temperatures inside a cold frame can be up to 20°F warmer than the air outside. Heating coils, cables, and pads are also available to keep soil warm regardless of temperatures.

A cold frame is very useful for early planting of annuals and seeds. It protects tender plants in winter, helps cuttings root faster, and raises many kinds of delicate, hard-to-start plants that would otherwise be impossible to grow.

This attached lean-to greenhouse provides a head start for plants while trees outside have yet to bud. A matching brick wall ties the structure into the overall design of the house.

the extra capacity needed for greenhouse heating. If your central heating system is not powerful enough or easy to hook up or if you have a freestanding greenhouse, an independent heating system is required.

Electric heaters are convenient and easy to install (though they can be expensive to run). They should have a thermostat and a built-in circulation fan to ensure even heat distribution and accurate temperature control. For a small greenhouse, one or two space heaters may be sufficient. Alternatives include self-contained heaters that burn natural gas or fuel oil. With these units, a separate thermostat located at plant level provides good temperature control. Fuel-burning heaters should always be vented to the outside.

The amount of heat required depends on outside temperatures, greenhouse size, and the type of glazing used.

Shading and shutters are also important for keeping the greenhouse cool on hot days and warm on cold nights. Commercial shading material is lightweight black or green fabric designed to protect plants from the hottest sun. It comes in a variety of shapes and sizes, and often has string attached at the corners so it can be pulled over the house and fastened. Shutters are insulating panels installed inside or outside on cold nights to keep the greenhouse warm. Check with a greenhouse supplier for more information about these products.

Ventilation: A steady supply of fresh air is vital for good plant health. Hand-operated roof vents, usually in conjunction with an exhaust fan, are one means of greenhouse ventilation, but require frequent temperature adjustments so that plants don't get too hot or cold. Automatic ventilation systems triggered by a thermostat are a convenient alternative. In both cases, a fan is installed at one end of the greenhouse and the inlet vent is located at the other (base vents near the ground may also be incorporated). A small fan should also be installed

to move air around when vents are closed. In an automated system, the fan and inlet vent are activated when the temperature rises to a preset level. Hot air is then expelled and fresh air enters through the vents.
Water: For the greenhouse grower, watering is the most demanding and difficult chore. You may be able to get by using a garden hose, but it is easier to have a separate faucet next to the greenhouse. Running a permanent water supply to a free-standing greenhouse requires digging a trench for the supply pipe below the frost line.

A sprinkler system is a useful addition. It can be as simple as perforated pipe set a few feet above the plant benches and connected to the water supply valve. Other options include timer-controlled mist systems and evaporative coolers that circulate moist air.

ANATOMY OF A GREENHOUSE

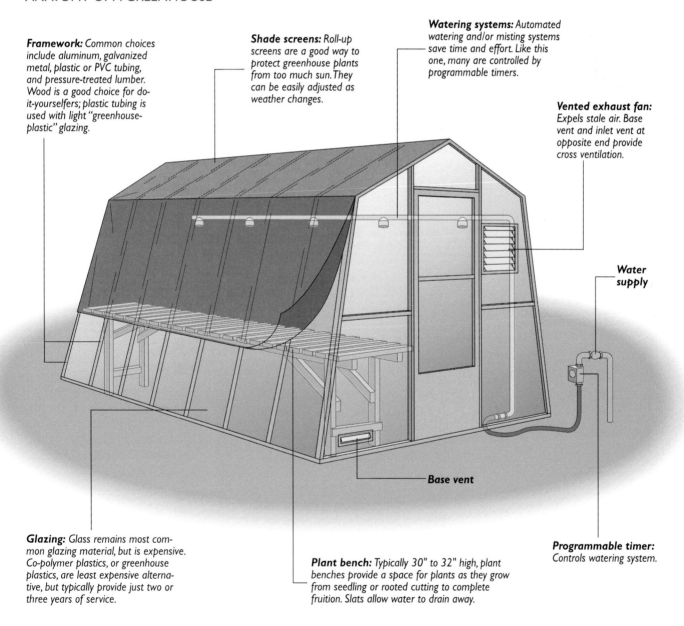

Framework: *Common choices include aluminum, galvanized metal, plastic or PVC tubing, and pressure-treated lumber. Wood is a good choice for do-it-yourselfers; plastic tubing is used with light "greenhouse-plastic" glazing.*

Shade screens: *Roll-up screens are a good way to protect greenhouse plants from too much sun. They can be easily adjusted as weather changes.*

Watering systems: *Automated watering and/or misting systems save time and effort. Like this one, many are controlled by programmable timers.*

Vented exhaust fan: *Expels stale air. Base vent and inlet vent at opposite end provide cross ventilation.*

Water supply

Base vent

Glazing: *Glass remains most common glazing material, but is expensive. Co-polymer plastics, or greenhouse plastics, are least expensive alternative, but typically provide just two or three years of service.*

Plant bench: *Typically 30" to 32" high, plant benches provide a space for plants as they grow from seedling or rooted cutting to complete fruition. Slats allow water to drain away.*

Programmable timer: *Controls watering system.*

Sheds

With a shed in your garden, you can keep outdoor gear near to where you use it while clearing space in the garage, attic, and basement.

Depending on how industrious you are, you can erect a metal shed frame from a kit, assemble the parts of a prefab unit, or build your own shed from scratch. Shed kits and prefab units are discussed on page 101, while an overview of shed construction is included on the page opposite.

LOCAL CODES

Sheds can be simple or elaborate, depending on your needs, space, and budget. However, before setting your sights on a particular structure, check with your local building department about whether you need a permit and what codes will affect the building. Detached sheds are often subject to requirements regarding minimum setbacks from property lines. You may also face limits installing water and electrical lines or be required to build your shed with fire-retardant materials.

PLANNING SHED STORAGE

The key to effective storage in a limited space such as a shed is to keep small objects off the floor. Floor space is valuable and you'll want to save it for ease of access and for heavy equipment. You can fasten cabinets, shelves, tools racks, and workbenches to the framing members in a wood shed. If you don't want to use the manufacturer's storage accessories for a metal shed, you may want to build a wooden frame inside it.

To help you plan your shed's interior, consider the following tips:
• Old kitchen cabinets or counters with built-in drawers are great for a mid-size shed.
• Garden poisons should be locked in a cabinet out of children's reach.
• If you have a hinged door that swings out, install narrow shelves on the back of the door.
• Industrial metal shelves can be used in a shed; they won't warp from dampness, but they may rust.

To blend into its environment, the look of this shed takes its cue from the design of the house it accompanies, incorporating the same roofing material, siding, and paint-color scheme.

Shed Construction Basics

The structure of a basic shed, like the one shown at right, is much the same as that for a house. Both are typically platform-frame buildings.

The "platform" in platform-frame construction consists of the foundation and the floor structure. Generally, the floor of a shed is composed of joists supported by skids that rest on the ground, a concrete slab, or piers such as the one shown below. Proper joist span varies according the thickness of the structural plywood used for the floor. The walls are built up from the floor, and the framing is completed with ceiling and roof framing members. The walls, ceiling, and roof are composed almost entirely of 2x dimensional lumber, fastened with nails and sometimes metal framing connectors.

Over the frame, sheathing—usually plywood—provides a base for exterior siding. Roofing felt provides moisture protection between the sheathing and roofing material.

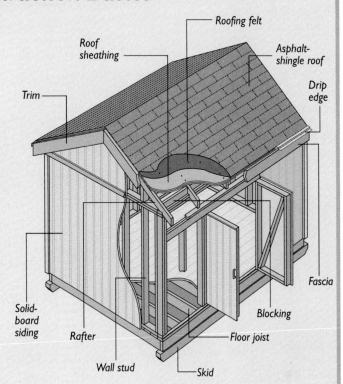

Roof sheathing — Roofing felt — Asphalt-shingle roof — Drip edge — Trim — Fascia — Solid-board siding — Rafter — Wall stud — Skid — Floor joist — Blocking

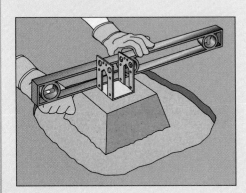

Casting the piers
The simplest method for building concrete foundations is to cast a footing and set a precast concrete block on top of it (left). The skid that supports the shed's floor joists rests in the post anchor on top of the pier (in some cases, the skid will rest on a short post in the post anchor).

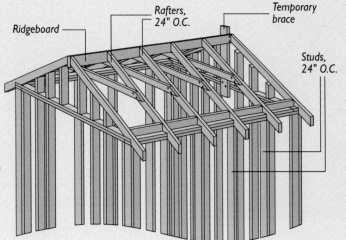

Ridgeboard — Rafters, 24" O.C. — Temporary brace — Studs, 24" O.C.

Framing the shed
A shed requires much the same structure as any other framed building; the rafters, joists, and studs can be spaced on 24-inch centers. The lighter stresses allow the use of 2x4s instead of sturdier members used in house construction. The exception is the floor joists, which should not be smaller than 2x6s.

Prefab sheds need not be eyesores. This wooden model is both attractive and functional. Its double doors and wide ramp allow easy entry for larger pieces of equipment such as ride-on lawn mowers.

The style of this customized shed, along with an antique wheelbarrow, adds country charm to the space, proving that sheds can be as decorative as they are functional.

SHED KITS

If you've decided that you need a shed but don't feel confident about building a wooden structure from scratch, you have the option of buying a shed kit. Shed kits are available in wood and metal designs at many hardware stores and home and garden centers as well as through mail order. They can be ordered to suit your construction abilities, budget, and setting. Metal sheds tend to be easier to put up, although they are available in a limited number of designs; differences are generally restricted to size, roof style, door systems, and color. In contrast, wood-shed kits are available in a wide variety of styles, but require greater building skills. Often, existing structures will determine

what type of shed you should use. If your house is wood, for example, a wooden shed is an excellent choice.

Metal-shed kits are almost always sold as complete packages, containing sheet-metal panels, framing sections, trim, and hardware—screws, bolts, washers, and so on. Assembly requires a few basic tools.

The initial step in assembling a metal shed is to connect the framing sections and bolt the wall panels in place. The gabled roof and door are added next. The last step is anchoring the shed to a prepared base or directly to the ground, depending on the design.

When buying a wood-shed kit, check carefully to see what kind of skills you'll

need to complete the project successfully. Some kits represent a full-scale construction project, with specialized tools and skills required. Other kits are just as complete as their metal counterparts.

An advantage of wooden sheds is that you can customize the structure—both inside and out. Inside you can fasten shelves, hooks, hangers, and work surfaces to the walls, while outside you can chose paint colors, trim, and other finish materials to better suit the setting.

While the building process varies according to the shed plans, the same basic shed-construction steps outlined on page 99 apply in the construction of a wood-shed kit.

A Place for
RECREATION

Outdoor living spaces aren't just for sitting and relaxing. As any parent will testify, they're also for playing. If you have young children, it's a great idea to incorporate a special recreation area into your backyard design. This will encourage your youngsters to play at home and help save your plant beds from destruction by little feet. The following chapter includes tips for setting aside a designated area for children, and provides building plans for a jungle gym and playhouse. Grown-ups like to have fun, too: At the end of this chapter, you'll find information about the layout and space requirements for three popular games— badminton, croquet, and volleyball.

Play Spaces

In warmer months, children naturally spend more of their time outdoors, playing sports and games of all kinds. If you have youngsters, converting a part of your living space into a play area is virtually a must if you want to keep them in the yard and safely entertained.

When you design an outdoor recreation space for children, you'll have to consider the kind of play equipment you want to include (if any) and the best place to set it up. As with other living spaces, the key here is to focus on your needs—or in this case, the needs of your youngsters. There is a vast array of equipment to choose from, ranging from traditional swings and slides to the most elaborate multi-purpose play structures imaginable. Some of these items you can build yourself from scratch if you have the desire and the abilities—

a tire swing or a sandbox are ideal basic projects. Slightly more skilled homeowners may want to take on a more involved project for their children. Two such projects, the backyard gym on page 104 and the storybook cottage on page 106, are provided in this chapter.

If the prospect of building from scratch is less than appealing, a wide assortment of play structures can be bought in kit form and put together following the manufacturer's instructions. Some companies will have employees come to your home to assemble the structure in your chosen location, although this option can be expensive.

The layout considerations for recreation areas are much the same as for any other space, with a few exceptions. You'll want to provide adequate shade and shelter, and you'll want to arrange the space in

a way that does not monopolize the whole yard. Spaces for younger children should be located in an area you can see from the house, allowing you to be inside watching while your youngsters are at play. Check the views from various windows of the home. Mark this information on your base map and keep it in mind as you draw up your plan.

Play areas generally need hardy groundcover in order to withstand the wear and tear of children's outdoor activities. Some sturdy grasses include bluegrass, bluegrass-rye mixture, and bermuda grass. In some cases, grass is not the best choice—it wears out and is difficult to cut around equipment. See the sidebar below for information on other suitable groundcovers. If possible, avoid putting fragile plants near the play space—they likely won't survive.

Groundcovers for Recreational Areas

While grass is attractive and provides an effective cushion, it may wear out over time and can be difficult to trim around play equipment. Here are some other popular play-area groundcovers.

Wood chips and sand: Wood chips are soft and giving, but can lose their cushioning effect when mixed with soil or wet with rain. Sand is inexpensive but messy. Maintain a layer of wood chips about 6 inches deep or a sand layer 12 inches deep. Expect to re-level both sand and wood chips from time to time.

Pea gravel: To avoid having sand tracked indoors, stray wood chips strewn about the lawn, and grass stains on clothes, pea gravel may be an ideal solution. It doesn't stain, isn't costly, and doesn't have to be replaced as often as some of the other alternatives. The only drawbacks of a 3-inch-deep bed of gravel are that younger children may find it a bit difficult to walk or run on these stones; and some love to throw it at others or onto the lawn.

Other options: Some city playgrounds have begun to use cleaned pieces of shredded tires as playground cushioning material. This is an effective and environmentally sound option. Rice hulls may also prove to be an effective, albeit unusual, cushioning material. If you live near a rice-growing region, you may be able to buy hulls from a garden supplier. Soft and attractive, the hulls do have one drawback—they blow away more readily than other covers; limit this by dampening them occasionally.

Backyard Gym

This project provides youngsters with three safe ways to play. Use the instructions and illustrations that follow to help you build. Use galvanized 3-inch nails for fastening unless otherwise indicated. Note: Posthole locations can affect the size of components. Erect posts and check measurements before cutting other components.

POSTS

Cut seven sandbox posts (B), then bevel and dado the tops of the six remaining tall posts (A), if desired. Dig each posthole at least 8 inches wide. You'll need a helper to set the posts; make sure they're plumb and aligned. Then, pour concrete into the holes.

PLATFORM, RAMP, SLIDE, AND RAILINGS

Put together the platform first, mounting two outside joists (I) to posts 52 inches above the ground with 3½-inch lag screws,

then secure the center joist (I) and cross joists (H) with 3½-inch nails. Nail the platform boards to the joists with 3½-inch nails and attach the platform beam to the posts with 6-inch lag screws. To build the ramp, set one support (M) against the platform at the desired angle, mark the angle on the support, and cut the board at the line. Saw a matching angle on the other support. Attach them to the platform with 3½-inch lag screws. Nail ramp boards (K) to the supports, then attach ramp cleats (N). To make the slide, lay the slide core pieces (X) on the metal and bend the metal over the ends. Build the slide cradle, nailing slide cleats (P) to the outside slide rails (O). Then, attach slide cleats (Q) for the lower bend. Join the two sides of the cradle with slide

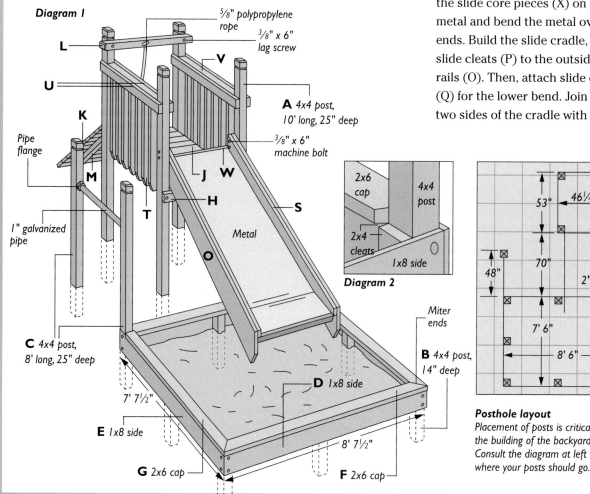

Diagram I

L

U

K

Pipe flange

M

1" galvanized pipe

T

C 4x4 post, 8' long, 25" deep

E 1x8 side

7' 7½"

G 2x6 cap

⅝" polypropylene rope

⅜" x 6" lag screw

V

A 4x4 post, 10' long, 25" deep

⅜" x 6" machine bolt

J W

H

S

Metal

O

D 1x8 side

8' 7½"

F 2x6 cap

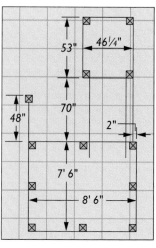

2x6 cap

4x4 post

2x4 cleats

1x8 side

Diagram 2

Miter ends

B 4x4 post, 14" deep

53"

46¼"

48"

70"

2"

7' 6"

8' 6"

Posthole layout
Placement of posts is critical to the building of the backyard gym. Consult the diagram at left to plot where your posts should go.

crosspieces (R). With a helper, hoist the cradle into position atop the platform and adjust it to the desired angle. Mark and cut the outside rails so they sit flush with the inside edges of the posts. Hang the cradle with machine bolts and nail the toe guard (W) in place. Secure the slide in the cradle with 3½-inch nails driven through crosspieces into cleats, then add inside rails (S). Install railings (U), then add uprights, and railing caps with 3½-inch nails.

SANDBOX

Fasten the sides to the posts with countersunk 2½-inch lag screws, then add the mitered caps. Where the caps meet the chinning-bar post, add 2x4 cleats (see Diagram 2).

FINISHING UP

Attach the rope and chinning bar, then sand all surfaces smooth. Finish the whole structure with preservative.

Design: Playscapes by Kelly

CUTTING AND MATERIALS LIST

A	**Platform posts**	Four 4x4s @ 10'
B	**Sandbox posts**	Seven 4x4s @ 21¼"
C	**Chin-bar posts**	Two 4x4s @ 8'
D	**Sandbox sides**	Two 1x8s @ 10'
E	**Sandbox sides**	Two 1x8s @ 8'
F	**Cap material**	Two 2x6s @ 10'
G	**Cap material**	Two 2x6s @ 8'
H	**Platform joist**	Two 2x6s @ 46¼"
I	**Platform joist**	Three 2x6s @ 53"
J	**Platform board**	Ten 2x6s @ 39¼"
K	**Ramp board**	Twelve 2x6s @ 46¼"
L	**Platform beam**	One 4x4 @ 55"
M	**Ramp support**	Two 4x4s cut to size
N	**Ramp cleat**	Three 2x6s @ 24"
O	**Outside slide rail**	Two 2x12s cut to size
P	**Slide cleat**	Two 2x4s @ 8'
Q	**Slide cleat**	Two 2x4s @ 12"
R	**Slide crosspiece**	Six 2x6s @ 36"
S	**Inside slide rail**	Two 2x6s cut to size
T	**Railing upright**	Thirteen 2x4s @ 37½"
U	**Railing**	Four 2x6s @ 53"
V	**Railing caps**	Two 2x4 @ 46"
W	**Toe guard**	One 2x6 @ 39¼"
X	**Slide core pieces**	¾" @ 4' x 8'
Lag screws and washers		Two @ ⅜" x 6", eleven @ ⅜" x 3½", twenty-four @ ⅜" x 2½"
Machine bolts, washers, and locknuts		Four @ ⅜" x 6"
Sheet metal		Galvanized @ 26 gauge
Metal pipe		Flanged @ 1" diameter
Common nails		5 lbs @ 3½", 1lb @ 3"
Polypropylene rope		12' @ ⅝" diameter
Premixed concrete		Ten bags
Wood preservative		

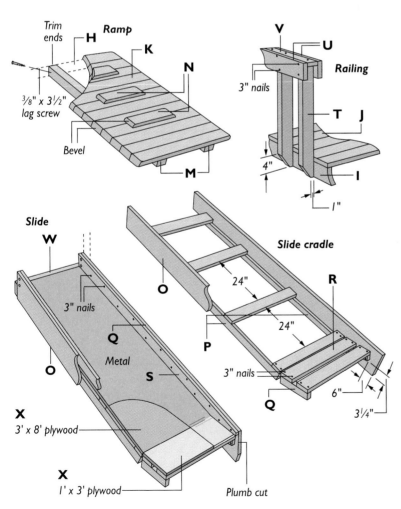

Trim ends — **H** **Ramp** **K**

⅜" x 3½" lag screw

Bevel

N

M

V **U**

Railing

3" nails

T **J**

4"

1"

I

Slide

W

3" nails

O

Q

Metal

O

S

X

3' x 8' plywood

X

1' x 3' plywood

Slide cradle

24"

24"

R

P

3" nails

Q

6"

3¼"

Plumb cut

Storybook Cottage

Roof framing

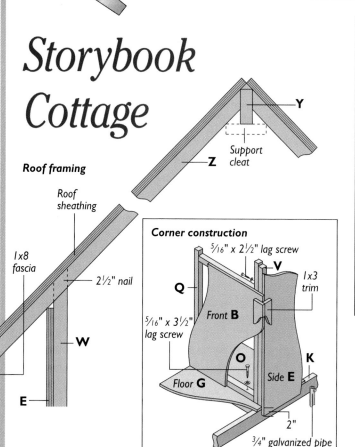

Support cleat

Y

Z

Roof sheathing

1x8 fascia

2½" nail

W

E

Corner construction

⁵⁄₁₆" x 2½" lag screw

V

Q

1x3 trim

Front **B**

⁵⁄₁₆" x 3½" lag screw

O

K

Floor **G**

Side **E**

2"

¾" galvanized pipe

A playhouse can be a ticket to a world of fun and imagination. For a carpenter with moderate to advanced skills, this charming cottage takes just a few weekends to build.

BUILDING PLANS

The illustrations here and on the following pages provide various views of the cottage construction details, from flooring to rafter construction.

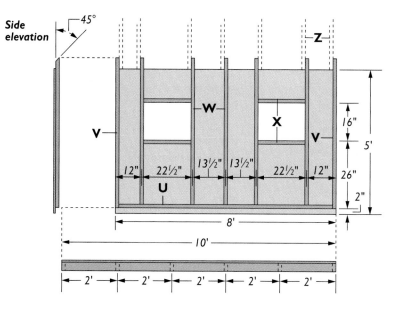

Side elevation

45°

Z

W

X

V

V

16"

5'

26"

2"

12"   22½"   13½" 13½"   22½"   12"

U

8'

10'

2'   2'   2'   2'   2'

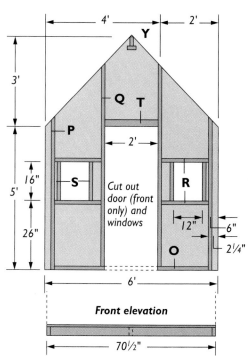

4'   2'

Y

3'

Q   T

P

2'

16"

5'

S

Cut out door (front only) and windows

R

12"

6"

2¼"

26"

O

6'

Front elevation

70½"

CUTTING AND MATERIALS LIST

A, B	Front pieces	One each ⅝" plywood @ 4' x 8', as shown
C, D	Back pieces	One each ⅝" plywood @ 4' x 8', as shown
E	Side pieces	Four ⅝" plywood @ 48" x 5"
F	Floor pieces	Four ⅝" plywood @ 45" x 35¼"
G	Floor pieces	One ⅝" plywood @ 24" x 70½"
H	Roof pieces	Two ⅝" plywood @ 12" x 96"
I	Roof pieces	Two ⅝" plywood @ 18" x 60"
J	Roof pieces	Two ⅝" plywood @ 48" x 96"
K	Floor pieces	Two 2x4s @ 10'
L	Floor pieces	Six 2x4s @ 67½"
M	Floor pieces	Three 2x4s @ 22½"
N	Floor pieces	Two 2x4s @ 21¾"
O, U	Sole plates	Two 2x2s each @ 64½" and 93"
P, Q	Wall studs	Four 2x2s each, cut to size
R, S	Framing pieces	Eight 2x2s each @ 19½" and 16"
T	Door header	One 2x4 @ 22½"
V	Outside studs	Four 2x2s @ 62¼"
W	Inside studs	Ten 2x2s @ 60¾"
X	Framing pieces	Eight 2x2s @ 21"
Y	Ridgeboard	One 2x4 @ 8'
Z	Rafters	Fourteen 2x2s @ 58½"
Fascia boards		Two 1x8s @ 10' Four 1x6s @ 12'
Slide, door, and window trim		Five 1x4s @ 10' Eight 1x4s @ 8'
Door frame		Six 1x3s @ 8'
Corner trim boards and window frames		Twelve 1x3s @ 6' Two 1x2s @ 8'
Vertical battens (front and back walls)		One 1x2 @ 6'
Acrylic sheets		3/16", to fit windows
Nails, hardware, and finish as required		

A playhouse—a room of one's own—can be the ticket to a world of fun and fantasy. This model is built from 2x2 and 2x4 framing and plywood—either AC exterior for all surfaces or with rough-sawn, prestained plywood for the walls. Floor framing should be made from foundation-grade treated lumber, heartwood redwood, or another naturally rot-resistant species. Use construction-grade Douglas fir for pieces O to Z and grade 2 or better for the fascias, trim, door and window frames, and vertical battens. The details and finishing touches can be as fancy or as plain as you like. For instance, you can omit the rear windows if you will be placing the cottage against a row of trees at the border of your yard.

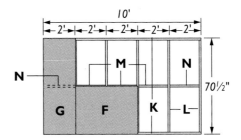

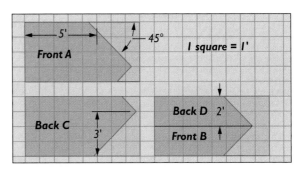

Details of floor and plywood sheathing
The diagrams above show how to construct the floor platform (upper) and how to make the angle cuts in the plywood pieces for the front and back of the cottage (lower). The side pieces of plywood sheathing are rectangular and need no angle cuts.

Storybook Cottage *continued* ▶

A PLACE FOR RECREATION

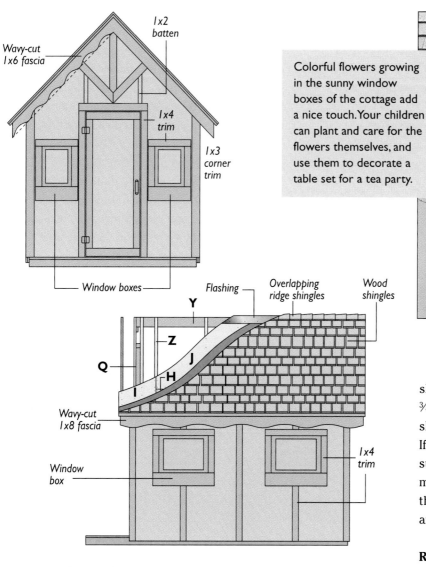

Wavy-cut
1x6 fascia

1x2
batten

1x4
trim

1x3
corner
trim

Window boxes

Flashing

Overlapping
ridge shingles

Wood
shingles

Y

Z

J

Q

H

I

Wavy-cut
1x8 fascia

Window
box

1x4
trim

Colorful flowers growing in the sunny window boxes of the cottage add a nice touch. Your children can plant and care for the flowers themselves, and use them to decorate a table set for a tea party.

To keep the cottage from shifting, stake the corners with ¾-inch pipe and lag screws as shown in the detail on page 106. If your yard slopes, you could substitute 2x6 floor framing members for the floor and level the structure as required on posts and concrete piers.

ADDING TRIM

Once the basic structure of the cottage is completed, add the door and windows *(opposite)*, then the trim *(above)* to provide the final decorative touches.

RAISING THE WALLS

Mark the positions of wall framing pieces O through X on the inside surfaces of the plywood walls. Cut the framing pieces and nail them together at the various connections using 3½-inch nails. Temporarily tack the framework to the plywood; turn the assembly over and nail through the plywood into the framing with 2-inch nails spaced every 12 inches.

CONSTRUCTING THE FLOOR

Nail the floor framing pieces K, L, M, and N together with 3½-inch nails. Add the plywood flooring pieces F and G, centering the panel edges over the framing pieces, then nail every 6 inches around the perimeter and every 12 inches along intermediate supports with 2-inch nails.

CUTTING DOOR AND WINDOW OPENINGS

Use a saber saw, circular saw, or keyhole saw to cut the door and window openings. Set the door panel aside.

ATTACHING WALLS TO FLOOR

With a helper, position one side wall on the floor. Hold the wall plumb, then drill pilot holes in the sole plate about every 32 inches and attach the wall to the floor with $\frac{5}{16}$- x $3\frac{1}{2}$-inch lag screws. Then, position the back wall, drill pilot holes in the corner studs, and secure the studs together with $\frac{5}{16}$- x $2\frac{1}{2}$-inch lag screws. Now, add the remaining walls.

FRAMING THE ROOF

Add support cleats for the ridgeboard (Y) at the roof peak, as shown on page 106. Then, nail Y to the front and back walls with $3\frac{1}{2}$-inch nails. Cut both ends of rafters (Z) at a 45° angle, then face-nail

each one to the stud on the ridgeboard. Add roof sheathing H, I, and J using 2-inch nails every 6 inches along the edges, every 12 inches everywhere else.

SHINGLING THE ROOF

Use roofing nails that are short enough not to poke through the underside. Begin at the eaves and work upward. Allow a 5-inch exposure for asphalt shingles and a $3\frac{3}{4}$-inch exposure for 16-inch wood shingles. Offset the joints.

ADDING TRIM AND EXTRAS

Add flashing at the ridge, then install the overlapping ridge shingles as shown in the illustrations on the page opposite.

Cut the wavy-edged fascia boards for the roof and trim them to length. Nail the 1x8 boards to the rafter ends and drive 2-inch screws through the sheathing to secure them. At the front and back, clamp the 1x6s in place and

screw down through the roof. Where they meet in the center, add a nailing cleat. Then, nail the pieces together at the corners.

DOORS AND WINDOWS

Use the reserved plywood panel to build the doors and windows. The design is entirely up to you. Some ideas are shown below. Hang the doors and windows with brass or galvanized butt hinges.

FINISHING TOUCHES

Caulk all the seams carefully and allow the caulk to dry before proceeding. You can then paint or stain the walls. Paint the trim pieces to match the cottage and attach them to the structure. Make the window boxes from plywood scraps, then secure them with carriage bolts.

Design: Don Vandervort

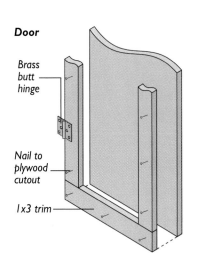

Door

Brass butt hinge

Nail to plywood cutout

1x3 trim

Window options

$\frac{3}{16}$" acrylic

1x3 trim

$\frac{3}{16}$" dado

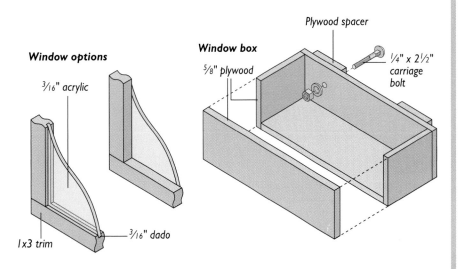

Plywood spacer

Window box

$\frac{5}{8}$" plywood

$\frac{1}{4}$" x $2\frac{1}{2}$" carriage bolt

Game Areas

Sports lovers with a large enough expanse of lawn can set out a professional-sized playing field for outdoor games or sports—turning part of the outdoor living area into a hub of competitive activity. The dimensions shown below are all regulation size. However, you can make them smaller if you don't have enough space.

If you do have the space but the land is uneven, you could consider grading part of your yard *(page 23)* to create a level playing field that could then be used for any one (or all three) of these popular outdoor sports.

As space requirements for even a modest-size playing field are considerable, be sure to include the area on your base map.

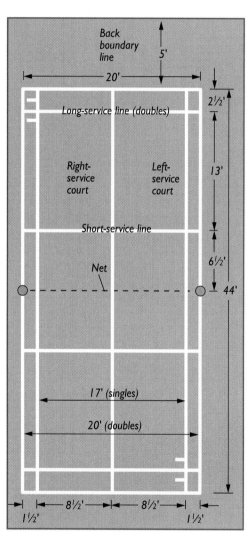

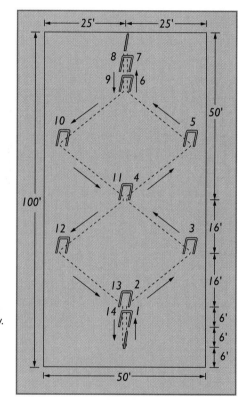

A badminton court
The illustration at left outlines the dimensions of a regulation-size badminton court. You may choose to alter the layout to suit the space available in your backyard. Plan to locate your court on flat, even ground, preferably with a grass surface.

A croquet field
At right is an illustration of a traditional croquet field, characterized by a nine-wicket, double diamond on which 14 wicket points are scored. (Balls pass through some wickets twice.) Beyond the layout, there need be no particular boundary. It is acceptable to lay out the wickets in a smaller pattern if the size of the playing area is too small.

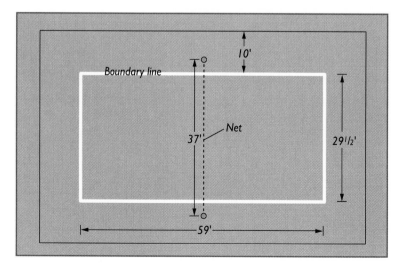

A volleyball court
Shown at right are dimensions of a regulation outdoor volleyball court as outlined by USA Volleyball. Use them as a guideline, altering the dimensions to fit your space. The court should be an expanse of level grass or sand (sand should be at least 18 inches deep). A flat, grassy surface around the court is best for safety. Net height should be 7 feet 11⅝ inches for men's or coed play and 7 feet 4¼ inches for women's play.

110

Project PLANS

Structures such as decks, gazebos, and sheds, along with outdoor furniture, are key elements of outdoor living areas. However, detailed plans and building instructions for such projects are beyond the scope of this book. In the pages that follow you will find a selection of practical, attractive outdoor structures for which you can order complete plan packages. There is also a small selection of outdoor-furniture projects. With these plans in hand, you can tackle a building project yourself—and experience the satisfaction of watching your creation take shape—or hire a professional carpenter or builder to do the work.

Pages 112 and 113 provide information about how to order plans, including how to determine the number of copies you will need, pricing, and an order form. Just choose the plan that's right for you from the descriptions beginning on page 114, then place your order.

Before You Order

Plan packages for the projects on the following pages include all of the information you'll need to successfully build the projects. When you order a plan set, you will receive complete, large-scale drawings, details, and specifications. The plans call-out part sizes, and most present detailed step-by-step instructions for assembly. Several offer plans for alternate sizes, enabling you to adapt the project to suit your outdoor living space. Before filling out the order form on the following page, note the information that follows.

HOW MANY PLAN SETS WILL YOU NEED?

Each plan package contains two complete sets of plans. Though a single set should suffice for a simple project such as a picnic table, the spare set may come in handy if you like to make modifications or scribble notes on your plans. For more complex designs, you may need several sets, particularly if you intend to obtain bids from two or three builders or carpenters.

If your building department requires a permit for a structure such as an attached deck or gazebo, figure you'll need one set each for yourself, the building department, and any builders or subcontractors involved in the project.

SERVICE AND PLAN DELIVERY

Company service representatives are available to answer questions and assist you in placing your order. Every possible effort is made to process and ship orders within 48 hours.

RETURNS AND EXCHANGES

Each set of project plans is specially printed and shipped to you in response to your specific order; consequently, requests for refunds cannot be honored. However, if the prints you order cannot be used, you may exchange them for another plan. For an exchange, you must return all sets of plans within 30 days. A nonrefundable service charge will be assessed for all exchanges; for more information, call our toll-free number (1-800-721-7027).

COMPLIANCE WITH LOCAL CODES AND REGULATIONS

Because of climatic, geographic, and political variations, building codes and regulations vary to some extent from one area to another. These plans are authorized for your use expressly conditioned on your obligation and agreement to comply strictly with all local building codes, ordinances, regulations, and requirements, including permits and inspections at the time of construction.

ARCHITECTURAL AND ENGINEER SEALS

With increased concerns about energy costs and safety, many cities and states now require that an architect or engineer review and "seal" a plan for a large structure, such as a house-attached multi-level deck, prior to construction. To find out whether this is a regulation in your area, contact your local building department.

LICENSE AGREEMENT, COPY RESTRICTIONS AND COPYRIGHT

When you purchase your plans, you are granted the right to use the documents to construct a single unit only.

All the plans in this publication are protected under the Federal Copyright Act, Title XVII of the United States Code and Chapter 37 of the Code of Federal Regulations. Each designer retains title and ownership of the original documents. The plans licensed to you cannot be used by or resold to any other person, copied, or reproduced by any means. If you require additional plans, you must order additional packets (again, each packet contains two complete sets of plans).

Complete the order form on the following page in three easy steps. Then mail in your order, or, for faster service, call our toll-free number (1-800-721-7027).

Ordering Plans

1. PLANS AND ACCESSORIES

Price Code	Description	Price
A	Small decks and projects	$12.95
B	Multi-level decks, arbors, and sheds	$15.95
C	Porches	$19.95
D	Gazebos	$24.95

Prices subject to change
Each plan package contains two sets of plans

2. SHIPPING AND HANDLING

Determine shipping and handling charges from the chart below.

Shipping and Handling Charges

Type of Service*	Plan Package	2 Plan Packages	3 Plan Packages
U.S. Regular	$4.95	$7.95	$9.95
U.S. Express	$12.50	$15.50	$18.50
Canada Regular	$7.45	$9.95	$12.45
Canada Express	$18.00	$20.50	$23.00

* U.S. Regular (4-6 working days) U.S. Express (2-3 working days)
Canada Regular (2-3 weeks) Canada Express (7-10 working days)

3. CUSTOMER INFORMATION

Choose the method of payment you prefer. Include a check, money order, or credit card information, complete the name and address portion, and mail the order form to:

Sunset/HomeStyles Plan Service
P.O. Box 75488
St. Paul, MN 55175-0488

**For faster service, call
1-800-721-7027**

PLAN CHECKLIST

Plan number(s) _____ Price code(s) _____

Number of packages _____ $ _____
(see chart at left)

Subtotal $ _____
Sales tax (Minnesota residents only, add 6.5%) $ _____
Shipping and handling $ _____
GRAND TOTAL $ _____

☐ Check/money order enclosed (in U.S. funds)
☐ VISA   ☐ MasterCard   ☐ AmEx   ☐ Discover

Credit card # _____

Exp. Date _____

Signature _____

Name _____

Address_____

City_____ State/Province_____

Country _____

Zip/Postal code_____

Daytime phone (____)_____

Please check if you are a contractor ☐

Mail form to: Sunset/HomeStyles Plan Service
P.O. Box 75488
St. Paul, MN 55175-0488

Or fax to: 651-602-5002

**FOR FASTER SERVICE,
CALL 1-800-721-7027
INTERNATIONAL CALL
651-602-5003**

Source code: SSPG

OCTAGON SUN DECK

SOM-2040
PRICE CODE A
- Plans for three different sizes:
  9', 12', and 16'
- Includes options to personalize
  the deck to suit your needs
- Step-by-step instructions

EASY FREESTANDING DECK

UC-2062-B
PRICE CODE A
- Three sizes: 8' X 12', 12' X 12',
  and 16' X 12'
- Easy-to-follow professional
  blueprints
- Dimensional drawings and details

PATIO DECK

Y-1366
PRICE CODE A
- Includes plans for four different sizes: 12' X 10', 12' X 14', 14' X 10', and 14' X 14'
- Details on benches, railing, and stairs
- Complete materials list

CASUAL CURVED DECK

SOM-2010
PRICE CODE A
- Four different deck sizes: 8' X 16', 10' X 16', 12' X 16', and 12' X 20'
- Planter and bench plans included
- Step-by-step instructions

BI-LEVEL DECK

Y-1375
PRICE CODE B
- Upper deck sizes: 12' X 12', 10' X 12', and 8' X 12'
- Lower deck sizes: 16' X 16', 10' X 12', and 8' X 10'
- Great for sloping lots

MID-LEVEL DECK

SOM-2070
PRICE CODE B
- Three different sizes included: 14' X 10', 16' X 12', and 20' X 12'
- Step-by-step instructions
- Includes options to personalize the deck

TRELLIS DECK

Y-1378
PRICE CODE B

- Overhead structure for welcome shade
- Four different sizes included: 16' X 20', 16' X 16', 14' X 20', and 14' X 16'
- Complete materials list

CUSTOM SPLIT-LEVEL DECK

SOM-2090
PRICE CODE B

- Plans include 12' X 8' upper-level deck, stair storage platform, and 22' X 16', 24' X 16', or 26' X 16' lower-deck options
- Bench and planter plans included
- Step-by-step instructions

SCREENED PORCH

HDA-9110
PRICE CODE C
- For porch 12'3" deep and 16'6" wide
- Step-by-step instructions
- Enjoy the warm weather in comfort
- Built-in plant shelves

SCREENED PORCH ADDITION

UC-6023-X
PRICE CODE C
- Porch size 16' X 12'
- Easy-to-follow professional blueprints
- Dimensional drawings and details

PORCH ADDITION

Y-347
PRICE CODE C
- A 12' X 12' room
- Design allows you to let the addition conform to the siding on your home
- Detailed step-by-step instructions

SHED-ROOF SCREENED PORCH

G-90012
PRICE CODE C
- Includes plans for six different sizes: 8' X 12', 8' X 16', 10' X 12', 10' X 16', 12' X 12', and 12' X 16'
- 4/12 pitch roof attaches to side or roof of house
- Side door and stair plans included

8-FOOT GAZEBO

Y-1691
PRICE CODE D
- 11' high, 8' wide across sides
- Airy design with elevated floor
- Materials list and detailed
  instructions

NOSTALGIC GAZEBO

SOM-8020
PRICE CODE D
- Plans for three different sizes:
  9', 12', and 16'
- Elegant design for use throughout
  the seasons
- Step-by-step instructions

CLASSIC GAZEBO

HPM-1601
PRICE CODE D
- 16' across the floor
- Detailed materials list
- Construction guidelines

SIMPLY FANCY GAZEBO

G-90018
PRICE CODE D
- Three sizes included: 8' X 8', 10' X 10', and 12' X 12'
- Stair and railing details
- Rafter cutting templates

ADIRONDACK CHAIR

UC-2070-B

PRICE CODE A

- Easy-to-follow professional blueprints
- Dimensional drawings and details

PORCH SWING

UC-2082-B

PRICE CODE A

- Traditional design
- Complete materials list

PICNIC TABLES

UC-2051-RB

PRICE CODE A

- Rectangular design 72" X 60" X 30"
- Octagonal design 56" X 56" X 30"

LEISURE BENCH

UC-2073-B

PRICE CODE A

- 5' bench and 4' table
- Dimensional drawings and details

SALT-BOX WORK SHED

HPM-1302
PRICE CODE B
- Shed is 10' X 14'
- Framing details and construction guidelines

CONTEMPORARY STORAGE SHED

HPM-1403
PRICE CODE B
- Shed is 8' X 10'
- Complete materials list and construction guidelines

SALT-BOX SHED

UC-2004-B
PRICE CODE B
- Includes plans for three sizes:
  8' X 8', 12' X 8', and 16' X 8'
- 8'2" height
- Dimensional drawings and details

YARD AND GARDEN SHED

SOM-6020
PRICE CODE B
- Three different sizes:
  8' X 12', 10' X 14', and 12' X 16'
- Concrete slab or wood floor
  options
- Step-by-step instructions

RAILROAD STATION PLAYHOUSE

Y-1676
PRICE CODE B

- 8' wide, 10' deep, 10' high
- Full-size plans and assembly drawings
- Finishing tips

TREELESS TREE HOUSE

Y-1837
PRICE CODE B

- 6' wide, 8' deep, 12' high
- Ladder to lookout balcony
- Sheltered sandbox below

ENTRANCE ARBORS

SOM-3001
PRICE CODE B

- Four different designs: Sunburst Arbor, Arched Arbor, Classic Arbor, and Sunrise Arbor
- Detailed architectural plans

LANDSCAPE ARBORS

SOM-3002
PRICE CODE B

- Four classic designs for the garden
- Includes enlarged structural details

TRELLIS PROJECTS

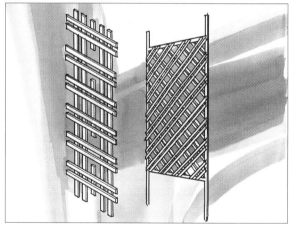

SOM-3003
PRICE CODE B

- 15 unique trellis designs, including privacy trellises and eave trellises
- Detailed step-by-step instructions

Index

Acknowledgments

The editors wish to thank the following:
Association of Professional Landscape Designers, Chicago, IL
Colorful Impressions Ltd., Dallas, TX
Richard Day, Palomar Mountain, CA
Frank S. Fitzgerald, Screen Manufacturers Association, Palm Beach, FL
Garden Concepts, Glenview, IL
Gwinnett Tech, Lawrenceville, GA
Hickson Corp., Smyrna, GA
Phifer Wire Products, Tuscaloosa, AL

Contributing Art Director:
Solange Laberge

Contributing Illustrator:
Panama Design
Charles Vinh

The following people also assisted in the preparation of this book:
Lorraine Doré, Pascale Hueber, Valery Pigeon-Dumas, Roberto Schulz, Michelle Turbide

Picture Credits

1 Philip Harvey
6 Jessie Walker
7 Crandall & Crandall
8 (lower) Ted Yarwood
8, 9 (upper) Ted Yarwood
9 (lower) Crandall & Crandall
10 Christopher Dew
11 (upper) Christopher Dew
11 (lower) Kenneth Rice
12 (upper) Jean-Claude Hurni
12 (lower) Phillip H. Ennis
13 (upper) Jean-Claude Hurni
13 (lower) Christopher Dew
14 (upper) Phillip H. Ennis
14 (lower) Crandall & Crandall
15 (upper) Crandall & Crandall
15 (lower) Jessie Walker
16 (left) Crandall & Crandall
16, 17 Ted Yarwood
17 (upper right) Peter Christiansen
18 Christopher Dew
20 Jean-Claude Hurni
34 Jean-Claude Hurni
35 Jean-Claude Hurni
41 Jean-Claude Hurni
43 (upper) Jessie Walker

43 (lower) Crandall & Crandall/Design: Brimer Construction
47 Phifer Wire Products
48 Jessie Walker
49 Jessie Walker
53 Kenneth Rice
54 Jessie Walker
55 Crandall & Crandall/Design: Michael Glassman & Associates
56 Peter Christiansen
57 Stuart Watson (3)
58 (upper) Crandall & Crandall
58 (lower) Crandall & Crandall/Design: Nick Williams & Associates
59 (both) Norman Plate
60 Crandall & Crandall/Design: John Herbst Jr. & Associates
61 Elaine Kilburne/Design: Rebecca Last
64 (upper) Jessie Walker
64 (lower) Peter Whiteley
65 Norman Plate (4)
66 Christopher Dew
67 (both) Jean-Claude Hurni
68 Peter Christiansen

71 Kenneth Rice
72 (upper) Phillip H. Ennis
72 (lower) Philip Harvey
74 Jean-Claude Hurni
78 Jean-Claude Hurni
79 Christopher Dew
81 Christopher Dew
83 (upper) Crandall & Crandall
83 (lower) Richard Nicol
84 Jean-Claude Hurni
85 Crandall & Crandall
86 Christopher Dew
88 Jessie Walker
89 Crandall & Crandall/Design: Blue Sky Designs
91 (both) Peter Whiteley
94 Christopher Dew
96 Crandall & Crandall
98 Crandall & Crandall/Design: James McIntire
100 Kenneth Rice
101 Jean-Claude Hurni
102 K. Bryan Swezey
106 Darrow M. Watt
108 Darrow M. Watt